Heavenly Artillery

Volume I

Damian C. Andre

For Jeremy

Also by Damian C. Andre

Mary's Psalter

Heavenly Artillery Vol II

Edited by Damian C. Andre

All Things Considered (Illustrated) by G. K. Chesterton

True Devotion to Mary (Illustrated) by St. Louis de Montefort

The Imitation of Christ (Illustrated) by Thomas à Kempis

Orthodoxy (Illustrated) by G. K. Chesterton

The Story Of A Soul: The Autobiography Of St. Therese Of Lisieux (Illustrated)

Table of Contents

INTRODUCTION

Its name deriving from the Latin word "novem," meaning "nine," a novena is nine days' private or public devotion in the Catholic Church to obtain special graces. Though they are not part of our liturgy and remain a "popular devotion" (a very few are prayed paraliturgically), they've been prayed since the very beginning of the Church – and before its official beginning: Mary and the Apostles prayed from His Ascension to the Pentecost, a period of nine days (Acts 1). Also, a nine-day period of supplication was a pagan Roman and Eastern practice, so novenas were easily accepted by the earliest converts in these lands.

The Christian and Jewish meaning of the number "9" entered into Christian thinking on the matter, as "9" was associated with suffering, grief, and imperfection, making it a fitting number for when "man's imperfection turned in prayer to God" (Catholic Encyclopedia). St. Jerome wrote that "the number nine in Holy Writ is indicative of suffering and grief" (Ezechiel, vii, 24).

Novenas, then, often, but not necessarily, have about them a sense of "urgency"; they are typically made for special intentions, one's own or another's ("I'll make a novena for you"). Novenas to certain Saints are often made according to that Saint's patronage; for ex., because of his New Testament letter encouraging Christians to persevere in the face of persecution, St. Jude is the patron of desperate situations and "hopeless" causes, so a person who finds himself or a loved one in a real tough bind might make a novena to St. Jude (by the way, it is traditional, after making a novena to St. Jude, to make a public expression of your gratitude. This is the reason for those mysterious thank you notes to St. Jude that you might see in your local newspaper's Classifieds section).

There are four main types of novenas (a novena may fit into more than one category):

- novenas of mourning, such as the novena made during the novemdiales – the nine day period following the death of a Pope

- novenas of preparation, or "anticipation," such as the Christmas or Easter Novenas

- novenas of prayer

- the indulgenced novenas

In some novenas, the same prayer is said each day for nine days, or sometimes 9 times in one day; others may have (or add) different prayers for each of the 9 prayer sessions. Some "novenas" aren't properly called "novenas" because the number nine plays no role in any way, but still retain the label. When a Novena is prayed in anticipation of a Feast, it is typically begun such that it ends the day before the Feast (I.e., to know when to start a Novena in anticipation of a Feast, count 10 days back from the Feast, with the Feast itself counting as "one.")

Be aware that some uneducated persons think about Novenas in a superstitious manner. Any Novena instructions that include words such as, "say this prayer for 9 consecutive days and your wish will be granted to you," or that describe the Novena as "never fail" in some sense that would lead one to believe that we have God at our beck and call rather than our being His humble servants – well, while the prayers themselves might (or might not) be OK, such instructions should be absolutely rejected.

Below is a selection of traditional Novenas. Most are written in the first person singular, but can easily be altered so they can be prayed in groups (change the "I's" to "we's" and "me's" to "us," etc.).

ADVENT NOVENA

Note: It is the general practice to start this Novena on St. Andrew's Feast day, November 30th.

The beautiful prayer that follows is traditionally said 15 days until Christmas. This prayer is very meditative, helpings us to increase our awareness of the real focus of Christmas and helping us to prepare ourselves spiritually for the coming of Jesus.

PRAYER

Hail and blessed be the hour and moment

In which the Son of God was born Of the most pure Virgin Mary

at midnight, in Bethlehem, in the piercing cold.

In that hour vouchsafe, I beseech Thee, O my God,

to hear my prayer and grant my desires,

[Make your request here...]

through the merits of Our Saviour Jesus Christ,

and of His Blessed Mother.

Amen.

My Christmas Pledge with Prayer to the Infant Jesus

I Promise...

1. To make my Christmas a holy day with Christ,

    not a holiday without Him.

2. To observe Christmas as the birthday of Christ,

not a day to give and receive material gifts.

3. To remember that the real symbols of Christmas are the Star, the Stable and the Crib,

   not Santa Claus and his reindeer.

4. To teach my children that "Santa Claus" is the nickname of St. Nicholas, who gave to the poor in honor of Christ.

 5. To help one poor family, in honor of Jesus, Mary and Joseph, the Holy Family of Bethlehem.

6. To send Christmas cards remindful of Him, the Infant Savior, not decorated only with candy canes, dogs, ribbons and wreaths.

7. To make room in my home for Him with a Christmas Crib to remind me that He was born in a stable.

8. During the Christmas season, in a special way, to honor Mary, His mother who kept the first Christmas vigil beside the manger.

9. To begin Christmas by leading my family to His altar to receive the Bread of Life.

10. Today and every day, to give "Glory to God in the highest" to work and pray for "Peace on earth to men of good will."

PRAYER TO THE INFANT JESUS

Come to me, O Divine Savior,

vouchsafe to be born in my heart.

Grant that, taught by Thine example,

and assisted by Thy grace,

I may be poor in spirit and humble of heart.

Keep me chaste and obedient.

I wish to live but for Thee,

and to do all things purely for love of Thee.

O Mary, my Advocate and Mother,

obtain by thy prayers forgiveness of my past offenses

and holy perseverance unto death.

St. Joseph, do thou also pray for me,

that I may become daily more pleasing to Jesus.

Amen.

ALL SOULS NOVENA

[Say once a day for nine days, starting on the 24th of October until the eve of All Souls Day.]

O God, the Creator and Redeemer of all the faithful,

grant to the souls of Thy servants and handmaids departed,

the remission of all their sins;

that through pious supplications

they may obtain the pardon they have always desired.

Who livest and reignest with God the Father

in the unity of the Holy Ghost,

God, world without end.

Amen

CHRISTMAS NOVENA #1

Hail, and blessed be the hour and moment

At which the Son of God was born

Of a most pure Virgin

At a stable at midnight in Bethlehem

In the piercing cold

At that hour vouchsafe, I beseech Thee,

To hear my prayers and grant my desires

(Mention your request[s] here).

Through Jesus Christ and His most Blessed Mother.

DAY ONE

God's Love Revealed In His Becoming Man.

Thought:

Because our first parent Adam had rebelled against God, he was driven out of paradise and brought on himself and all his descendants the punishment of eternal death.

But the son of God, seeing man thus lost and wishing to save him from death, offered to take upon Himself our human nature and to suffer death Himself, condemned as a criminal on a cross.

"But, My Son," we may imagine the eternal Father saying to Him, "think of what a life of humiliations and sufferings Thou wilt have to lead on earth.

Thou wilt have to be born in a cold stable and laid in a manger, the feeding trough of beasts.

While still an infant, Thou wilt have to flee into Egypt, to escape the hands of Herod. After Thy return from Egypt, Thou wilt have to live and work in a shop as a lowly servant, poor and despised. And finally, worn out with sufferings, Thou wilt have to give up Thy life on a cross, put to shame and abandoned by everyone."

"Father," replies the Son, "all this matters not. I will gladly bear it all, if only I can save man."

What should we say if a prince, out of compassion for a dead worm, were to choose to become a worm himself and give his own life blood in order to restore the worm to life?

But the eternal Word has done infinitely more than this for us. Though He is the sovereign Lord of the world, He chose to become like us, who are immeasurably more beneath Him than a worm is beneath a prince, and He was willing to die for us, in order to win back for us the life of divine grace that we had lost by sin.

When He saw that all the other gifts which He had bestowed on us were not sufficient to induce us to pray His love with love, He became man Himself and gave Himself all to us. "The Word was made flesh and dwelt among us;" "He loved us and delivered Himself up for us."

Prayer:

O Great Son of God,

Thou hast become man in order to make Thyself loved by men.

But where is the love that men give Thee in return?

Thou hast given Thy life blood to save our souls.

Why then are we so unappreciative that, instead of repaying Thee with love, we spurn Thee with ingratitude?

And I, Lord, I myself more than others have thus ill treated Thee.

But Thy Passion is my hope.

For the sake of that love which led Thee to take upon Thyself human nature and to die for me on the cross, forgive me all the offenses I have committed against Thee.

I love Thee, O Word Incarnate;

I love Thee, O infinite goodness.

Out of love for Thee, that I could die of grief for these offenses.

Give me, O Jesus, Thy love.

Let me no longer live in ungrateful forgetfulness of the love Thou bearest me.

I wish to love Thee always.

Grant that I may always preserve in this holy desire.

O Mary, Mother of God and my Mother, pray for me that thy Son may give me the grace to love Him always, unto death.

Amen.

SECOND DAY

God's Love Revealed In His Being Born An Infant.

Thought:

When the Son of God became man for our sake, He could have come on earth as an adult man from the first moment of of His human existence, as Adam did when he was created.

But since the sight of little children draws us with an especial attraction to love them, Jesus chose to make His first appearance on earth as a little infant, and indeed as the poorest and most pitiful infant that was ever born.

"God wished to be born as a little babe," wrote Saint Peter Chrysologus, "in order that He might teach us to love and not to fear Him."

The prophet Isaias had long before foretold that the Son of God was to be born as an infant and thus give Himself to us on account of the love He bore us: "A child is born to us, a son is given to us."

My Jesus, supreme and true God!

What has drawn Thee from heaven to be born in a cold stable, if not the love which Thou bearest us men?

What has allured Thee from the bosom of Thy Father, to place Thee in a hard manger?

What has brought Thee from Thy throne above the stars, to lay Thee down on a little straw?

What has led Thee from the midst of the nine choirs of angels, to set Thee between two animals?

Thou, who inflamest the seraphim with holy fire, art now shivering with cold in this stable!

Thou, who settest the stars in the sky in motion, canst not now move unless others carry Thee in their arms!

Thou, who givest men and beasts their food, has need now a little milk to sustain Thy life!

Thou, who art the joy of heaven, dost now whimper and cry in suffering!

Tell me, who has reduced Thee to such misery?

"Love has done it," says Saint Bernard.

The love which Thou bearest us men has brought all this on Thee.

Prayer:

O Dearest Infant!

Tell me, what hast Thou come on earth to do?

Tell me, whom art Thou seeking?

Yes, I already know.

Thou has come to die for me, in order to save me from hell.

Thou hast come to seek me, the lost sheep, so that, instead of fleeing from Thee any more,

I may rest in Thy loving arms.

Ah my Jesus, my treasure, my life, my love and my all!

Whom will I love, if not Thee? Where can I find a father, a friend, a spouse more loving and lovable than Thou art?

I love Thee, my dear God;

I love Thee, my only good.

I regret the many years when I have not loved Thee, but rather spurned and offended Thee.

Forgive me, O my beloved Redeemer; for I am sorry that I have thus treated Thee, and I regret it with all my heart.

Pardon me, and give me the grace never more to withdraw from Thee, but constantly to love Thee in all the years that still lie before me in this life.

My love, I give myself entirely to Thee; accept me, and do not reject me as I deserve.

O Mary, thou art my advocate.

By thy prayers thou dost obtain whatever thou wilt from thy Son.

Pray Him then to forgive me, and to grant me holy perseverance until death.

Amen.

THIRD DAY

The Life Of Poverty Which Jesus Led From His Birth.

Thought:

God so ordained that, at the time when His Son was to be born on this earth, the Roman emperor should issue a decree ordering everyone to go to the place of his origin and there be registered in the census.

Thus it came about that, in obedience to this decree, Joseph went to Bethlehem together with his virgin wife when she was soon to have her Child.

Finding no lodging either in the poor inn or in the other houses of the town, they were forced to spend the night in a cave that was used as a stable for animals, and it was here that Mary gave birth to the King of heaven.

If Jesus had been born in Nazareth, He would also, it is true, have been born in poverty; but there He would at least have had a dry room, a little fire, warm clothes and a more comfortable cradle.

Yet He chose to be born in this cold, damp cave, and to have a manger for a cradle, with prickly straw for a mattress, in order that He might suffer for us.

Let us enter in spirit into this cave of Bethlehem, but let us enter in a spirit of lively faith. If we go there without faith, we shall see nothing but a poor infant, and the sight of this lovely child shivering and crying on his rough bed of straw may indeed move us to pity.

But if we enter with faith and consider that this Babe is the very Son, God, who for love of us has come down on earth and suffers so much to pay the penalty for our sins, how can we help thanking and loving Him in return?

Prayer:

20

O Dear Infant Jesus, how could I be so ungrateful and offend Thee so often, if I realized how much Thou hast suffered for me?

But these tears which Thou sheddest, this poverty which Thou embracest for love of me, make me hope for the pardon of all the offenses I have committed against Thee.

My Jesus, I am sorry for having so often turned my back on Thee.

But now I love Thee above all else.

"My God and my all!"

From now on Thou, O my God, shalt be my only treasure and my only good.

With Saint Ignatius of Loyola I will say to Thee,

"Give me the grace to love Thee; that is enough for me."

I long for nothing else;

I want nothing else.

Thou alone art enough for me, my Jesus, my life, my love.

O Mary, my Mother, obtain for me the grace that I may always love Jesus and always be loved by Him.

Amen.

FOURTH DAY

The Life Of Humiliation Which Jesus Led From His Birth.

Thought:

The Sign which the angel gave the shepherds to help them find the newborn Savior, points to His lowliness:

"This shall be a sign to you: you will find an infant wrapped in swaddling clothes and lying in a manger."

No other newborn baby who was wrapped in poor swaddling clothes and lying in a manger, a feeding trough for animals, could be found anywhere else but in a stable.

Thus in lowliness the King of heaven, the Son of God, chose to be born, because He came to destroy the pride that had been the cause of man's ruin.

The prophets had already foretold that our Redeemer was to be treated as the vilest of men on earth and that He was to be overwhelmed with insults.

How much contempt had not Jesus indeed to suffer from men! He was called a drunkard, a trickster, a blasphemer and a heretic.

What ignominies He endured in His Passion!

His own disciples abandoned Him; one of them sold Him for thirty pieces of silver, and another denied having ever known Him.

He was led in bonds through the streets like a criminal; He was scourged like a slave, ridiculed as a fool, crowned with thorns as a mock king, buffeted and spit upon, and finally left to die, hanging on a cross between two thieves, as the worst criminal in the world.

"The noblest of all," says Saint Bernard, "is treated as the vilest of all."

But the Saint adds, "The viler Thou are treated, the dearer Thou art to me." The more I see Thee, my Jesus, despised and put to shame, the more dear and worthy of my love dost Thou become to me.

Prayer:

O Dearest Savior,

Thou hast embraced so many outrages for love of me, yet I have not been able to bear one word of insult without at once being filled with resentful thought,

I who have so often deserved to be trodden under foot by the demons in hell!

I am ashamed to appear before Thee, sinful and proud as I am.

Yet do not drive me from Thy presence,

O Lord, even though that is what I deserve.

Thou hast said that Thou wilt not spurn a contrite and humbled heart.

I am sorry for the offenses I have committed against Thee.

Forgive me, O Jesus. I will not offend Thee again.

For love of me Thou hast borne so many injuries; for love of Thee I will bear all the injuries that are done to me.

I love Thee, Jesus, who was despised for love of me.

I love Thee above every other good.

Give me the grace to love Thee always and to bear every insult for love of Thee.

O Mary, recommend me to Thy Son; pray to Jesus for me.

Amen.

FIFTH DAY

The Life Of Sorrow Which Jesus Led From His Birth.

Thought:

Jesus Christ could have saved mankind without suffering and dying. Yet, in order to prove to us how much He loved us, He chose for Himself a life full of tribulations.

Therefore the prophet Isaias called Him "a man of sorrows," His whole life was filled with suffering. His Passion began, not merely a few hours before His death, but from the the first moment of His birth.

He was born in a stable where everything served to torment Him.

His sense of sight was hurt by seeing nothing but the rough,

black walls of the cave;

His sense of smell was hurt by the stench of the dung from the beasts in the stable;

His sense of touch was hurt by the prickling straw on which He lay.

Shortly after His birth He was forced to flee into Egypt, where He spent several years of His childhood in poverty and misery.

His boyhood and early manhood in Nazareth were passed in hard work and obscurity.

And finally, in Jerusalem, He died on a cross, exhausted with pain and anguish.

Thus, then, was the life of Jesus but one unbroken series of sufferings, which were doubly painful because He had ever before His eyes all the sufferings He would have to endure till His death.

Yet, since our Lord had voluntarily chosen to bear these tribulations for our sake, they did not afflict Him as much as did the sight of our sins, by which we have so ungratefully repaid Him for His love towards us.

When the confessor of Saint Margaret of Cortona saw that she never seemed satisfied with all the tears she had already shed for her past sins, he said to her, "Margaret, stop crying and cease your lamenting, for God has surely forgiven you your offenses against Him."

But she replied, "Father, how can I cease to weep, since I know that my sins kept my Lord Jesus in pain and suffering during all His life?"

Prayer:

O Jesus, my sweet Love!

I too have kept Thee suffering through all Thy life.

Tell me, then, what I must do in order to win Thy forgiveness.

I am ready to do all Thou askest of me.

I am sorry, O sovereign Good, for all the offenses I have committed against Thee.

I love Thee more than myself, or a least I feel a great desire to love Thee.

Since it is Thou who hast given me this desire, do Thou also give me the strength to love Thee exceedingly.

It is only right that I, who have offended Thee so much, should love Thee very much.

Always remind me of the love Thou hast borne me, in order that my soul may ever burn with love of Thee and long to please Thee alone. O God of love, I, who was once a slave of hell, now give myself all to Thee.

Graciously accept me and bind me to Thee with the bonds of Thy love.

My Jesus, from this day and forever in loving Thee will I live, and in loving Thee will I die.

O Mary, my Mother and my hope, help me to love Thy dear God and mine.

This is the only favor I ask of thee, and through thee I hope to receive it.

Amen.

SIXTH DAY

God's Mercy Revealed In His Coming Down From Heaven To Save Us.

Thought:

Saint Paul says, "The goodness and kindness of God, our Savior, has appeared."

When the Son of God made Man appear on earth, then was it seen how great is God's goodness towards us.

Saint Bernard says that first God's power was manifested in the creation of the world and His wisdom in its conservation, but His merciful goodness was especially manifested later in His taking human nature on Himself, in order to save fallen mankind by His sufferings and death.

For what greater proof of His kindness towards us could the Son of God show us than in taking on Himself the punishment we had deserved?

See Him as a weak, newborn infant, wrapped in swaddling clothes and lying in a manger. Unable to move or feed Himself, He has need of Mary to give Him a little milk to sustain His life.

Or see Him again in Pilate's courtyard, tied with fast bonds to a column and there scourged from head to foot.

Behold Him on the way to Calvary, falling down from weakness under weight of the cross that He must carry.

Finally behold Him nailed to this tree of shame, on which He breathes His last amid pain and anguish.

Because Jesus Christ wished that His love for us should win all the love of our hearts for Himself, He would not send an angel to redeem us, but chose to come Himself, to save us by His Passion and death.

Had an angel been our redeemer, men would have had to divide their hearts in loving God as their Creator and an angel as their redeemer; but God, who desires men's whole hearts, as He was already their Creator, wished also to be their Redeemer.

Prayer:

O my Dear Redeemer!

Where should I be now, if Thou hadst not borne with me so patiently, but hadst called me from life while I was in the state of sin?

Since Thou hast waited for me till now, forgive me quickly, O my Jesus, before death finds me still guilty of so many offenses that I have committed against Thee.

I am so sorry for having vilely despised Thee, my sovereign Good, that I could die of grief.

But Thou canst not abandon a soul that seeks Thee.

If hitherto I have forsaken Thee,

I now seek Thee and love Thee.

Yes, my God, I love Thee above all else;

I love Thee more than myself.

Help me, Lord, to love Thee always during the rest of my life.

Nothing else do I seek of Thee.

But this I beg of Thee, this I hope to receive from Thee.

Mary, my hope, do thou pray for me.

If thou prayest for me,

I am sure of grace.

Amen.

SEVENTH DAY

Flight Of The Child Jesus Into Egypt.

Thought:

Although the Son of God came from heaven to save men, scarcely was He born when men began to persecute Him to death. Herod, fearing that this Child would deprive Him of his kingdom, seeks to destroy His life.

But St. Joseph is warned by an angel in a dream to take the Infant and His Mother and flee into Egypt. Joseph obeys at once, and tells Mary about it.

He takes the few tools of his trade, that he may use them to gain a livelihood in Egypt for himself and his poor family.

Mary wraps up a small bundle of clothes for the use of her little Son, and then, going to the crib, she says with tears in her eyes to her sleeping Child, "O my Son and my God! Thou hast come from heaven to save men; but hardly art Thou born when they seek to take Thy life."

Lifting Him meanwhile in her arms and continuing to weep, she sets out that same night with Joseph on the road to Egypt.

Let us consider how much these holy wanderers must have suffered in making so long a journey, deprived of every comfort.

The divine Child was not yet able to walk, and so Mary and Joseph had to take turns in carrying Him in their arms.

During their journey through the desert towards Egypt they had to spend several nights in the open air, with the bare ground for their bed.

The cold makes the Infant cry, and Mary and Joseph weep in pity for Him.

And who would not weep at thus seeing the Son of God poor and persecuted, a fugitive on earth, that he might not be killed by His enemies!

Prayer:

Dear Infant Jesus, crying so bitterly!

Well hast Thou reason to weep in seeing Thyself persecuted by men whom Thou lovest so much.

I, too, O God, have once persecuted Thee by my sins.

But Thou knowest that now I love Thee more than myself, and that nothing pains me more than the thought that I have so often spurned Thee, my sovereign Good.

Forgive me, O Jesus, and let me bear Thee with me in my heart in all the rest of the journey that I have still to make through life, so that together with Thee I may enter into eternity.

So often have I driven Thee from my soul by my sins.

But now I love Thee above all things, and I regret above other misfortunes that I have offended Thee.

I wish to leave Thee no more, my beloved Lord.

But do Thou give me the strength to resist temptations.

Never permit me to be separated from Thee again.

Let me rather die than ever again lose Thy good grace.

O Mary, my hope, make me always live in God's love and then die in loving Him.

Amen.

EIGHTH DAY

The Life Of The Child Jesus In Egypt And In Nazareth.

Thought:

Our Blessed Redeemer spent the first part of His childhood in Egypt, leading there for several years a life of poverty and humiliation.

In that land Joseph and Mary were foreigners and strangers, having there neither relatives nor friends.

Only with difficulty could they earn their daily bread by the labor of their hands.

Their home was poor, their bed was poor, their food was poor.

Here Mary weaned Jesus; dipping a piece of bread in water, she would put it in the sacred mouth of her Son.

Here she made His first little garments and clothed Him with them.

Here the Child Jesus took His first steps, stumbling and falling as other children first do.

Here too He spoke His first words, but stammeringly.

O wonder of wonders!

To what has not God lowered Himself for love of us!

A God stumbling and falling as He walks!

A God stammering in His speech!

Not unlike this was the poor and humble life that Jesus led in Nazareth after His return from Egypt. There, until He was thirty years old, He lived as a simple servant or workman in a carpenter shop, taking orders form Joseph and Mary.

"And He was subject to them."

Jesus went to fetch the water; He opened and closed the shop; He swept the house, gathered the fragments of wood for the fire, and toiled all day long, helping Joseph in his work.

Yet who is this? God Himself, serving as a apprentice! The omnipotent God, who with less than a flick of His finger created the whole universe, here sweating at the task of planing a piece of work!

Should not the mere thought of this move us to love Him?

Prayer:

O Jesus, my Savior!

When I consider how, for love of me,

Thou didst spend thirty years of Thy life hidden and unknown in a poor workshop, how can I desire the pleasures and honors and riches of the world?

Gladly do I renounce all these things, since I wish to be Thy companion on this earth, poor as Thou wast, mortified and humble as Thou wast, so that I may hope to be able one day to enjoy Thy companionship in heaven.

What are all the treasures and kingdoms of this world?

Thou, O Jesus, art my only treasure, my only Good!

I keenly regret the many times in the past when I spurned Thy friendship in order to satisfy my foolish whims.

I am sorry for them with all my heart.

For the future I would rather lose my life a thousand times than lose Thy grace by sin.

I wish never to offend Thee again, but always to love Thee.

Help me to remain faithful to Thee until death.

O Mary, thou art the refuge of sinners, thou art my hope.

Amen.

NINTH DAY

The Birth Of Jesus In The Stable Of Bethlehem.

Thought:

When the edict was issued by the emperor of Rome that everyone should go to his own city to be enrolled, Joseph and Mary went to be enrolled in Bethlehem.

How much the Holy Virgin must have suffered on this journey of four days, over mountainous road and in the wintertime, with its cold rain and wind!

When they arrived in Bethlehem, the time of Mary's delivery was near. Joseph, therefore, sought some lodging where she might give birth to her Child.

But because they were so poor, they were driven away from the houses and even from the public inn, where other poor people had found shelter.

So in that night they went a short way out of the town and there found a cave that was used as a stable, and here Mary entered. But Joseph said to his virgin wife, "Mary, how can you spend the night in this cold, damp cave and here give birth to your Child?"

Mary however replied, "Dear Joseph, this cave is the royal palace in which the King of kings, the Son of God, wishes to be born."

When the hour of her delivery had arrived, the holy Virgin, as she knelt in prayer, all at once saw the cave illumined with a dazzling light.

She lowered her eyes to the ground and there saw before her the Son of God now born on earth, a poor little Babe, crying and shivering in the cold.

Adoring Him as her God, she took Him to her breast and fondled Him.

Then she wrapped Him in swaddling clothes and laid Him on the straw of the manger that stood in the cave.

Thus did the Son of God choose to be born among us to prove His infinite love for us.

Prayer:

O Adorable Infant Jesus!

I should not have the boldness to cast myself at Thy feet, if I did not know that Thou Thyself invitest me to draw near Thee.

It is I who by my sins have made Thee shed so many tears in the stable of Bethlehem.

But since Thou hast come on earth to pardon repentant sinners, forgive me also, now that I am heartily sorry for having spurned Thee, my Savior and my God, who art so good and who hast loved me so much.

In this night, in which Thou bestowest great graces on so many souls, grant Thy heavenly consolation to this poor soul of mine also.

All that I ask of Thee is the grace to love Thee always, from this day forward, with all my heart.

Set me all on fire with Thy holy love. I love Thee,

O my God, who hast become a Babe for love of me.

Never let me cease from loving Thee ever more.

O Mary, Mother of Jesus and my Mother, thou canst obtain everything from thy Son by thy prayers.

This is the only favor I ask of Thee.

Do thou pray to Jesus for me.

Amen.

CHRISTMAS NOVENA #2

[Begins on December 16th.]

(Repeat the same prayer each day for 9 days.)

Divine Infant,

after the wonders of Your birth in Bethlehem, You wished to extend Your infinite mercy to the whole world by calling the Wise Men by heavenly inspiration to Your crib, which was in this way changed into a royal throne.

You graciously received those holy men who were obedient to the Divine call and hastened to Your feet.

They recognized and worshiped You as Prince of Peace, the Redeemer of mankind, and the very Son of God.

Show us also Your goodness and almighty power.

Enlighten our minds, strengthen our wills, and inflame our hearts to know You, to serve You, and to love You in this life, that we may merit to find our joy in You eternally in the life to come.

O Jesus, most powerful Child,

I implore You again to help me:

(State your intention here...)

Divine Child, great omnipotent God,

I implore through Your most Holy Mother's most powerful intercession, and through the boundless mercy of Your omnipotence as God, for a favorable answer to my prayer during this Novena.

Grant me the grace of possessing You eternally with Mary and Joseph and of adoring You with Your holy angels and saints.

CHRISTMAS NOVENA #3

[Say this Novena beginning on the 16 th of December and ending on the 24 th of December. This Novena, though it starts one day earlier than the O Antiphons, correlates with the O Antiphons in the titles used to address Jesus between the 17 th and the 24 the of December. It would, therefore, make a good Novena to pray when your family prays the O Antiphons.]

16 DECEMBER

O Shepherd that rulest Israel,

Thou that leadest Joseph like a sheep,

come to guide and comfort us.

Say 1 Our Father...

Say 1 Hail Mary...

Say 1 Glory Be...

17 DECEMBER

O Wisdom that comest out of the mouth of the Most High,

that reachest from one end to another,

and orderest all things mightily and sweetly,

come to teach us the way of prudence!

Say 1 Our Father...

Say 1 Hail Mary...

Say 1 Glory Be...

18 DECEMBER

O Adonai,

and Ruler of the house of Israel,

Who didst appear unto Moses in the burning bush,

and gavest him the law in Sinai,

come to redeem us with an outstretched arm!

Say 1 Our Father...

Say 1 Hail Mary...

Say 1 Glory Be...

19 DECEMBER

O Root of Jesse,

which standest for an ensign of the people,

at Whom the kings shall shut their mouths,

Whom the Gentiles shall seek,

come to deliver us,

do not tarry.

Say 1 Our Father...

Say 1 Hail Mary...

Say 1 Glory Be...

20 DECEMBER

O Key of David,

and Sceptre of the house of Israel,

that openeth and no man shutteth,

and shutteth and no man openeth,

come to liberate the prisoner from the prison,

and them that sit in darkness,

and in the shadow of death.

Say 1 Our Father...

Say 1 Hail Mary...

Say 1 Glory Be...

21 DECEMBER

O Dayspring,

Brightness of the everlasting light,

Son of justice,

come to give light to them that sit in darkness

and in the shadow of death!

Say 1 Our Father...

Say 1 Hail Mary...

Say 1 Glory Be...

22 DECEMBER

O King of the Gentiles,

yea, and desire thereof!

O Corner-stone, that makest of two one,

come to save man,

whom Thou hast made out of the dust of the earth!

Say 1 Our Father...

Say 1 Hail Mary...

Say 1 Glory Be...

23 DECEMBER

O Emmanuel,

our King and our Law-giver,

Longing of the Gentiles,

yea, and salvation thereof,

come to save us,

O Lord our God!

Say 1 Our Father...

Say 1 Hail Mary...

Say 1 Glory Be...

24 DECEMBER

O Thou that sittest upon the cherubim,

God of hosts, come, show Thy face,

and we shall be saved.

Say 1 Our Father...

Say 1 Hail Mary...

Say 1 Glory Be...

CORPUS CHRISTI NOVENA

(A Novena that honours the Body and Blood of Christ.)

I thank You, Jesus, my Divine Redeemer,

for coming upon the earth for our sake,

and for instituting the adorable Sacrament of the Holy Eucharist

in order to remain with us until the end of the world.

I thank You for hiding beneath the Eucharistic species Your infinite majesty and beauty,

which Your Angels delight to behold,

so that I might have courage to approach the throne of Your Mercy.

I thank You, most loving Jesus,

for having made Yourself my food,

and for uniting me to Yourself with so much love

in this wonderful Sacrament that I may live in You.

I thank You, my Jesus,

for giving Yourself to me in this Blessed Sacrament,

and so enriching it with the treasures of Your love

that You have no greater gift to give me.

I thank You not only for becoming my food

but also for offering Yourself as a continual sacrifice

to Your Eternal Father for my salvation.

I thank You, Divine Priest,

for offering Yourself as a Sacrifice daily upon our altars in adoration

and homage to the Most Blessed Trinity,

and for making amends for our poor and miserable adorations.

I thank You for renewing in this daily Sacrifice

the actual Sacrifice of the Cross offered on Calvary,

in which You satisfy Divine justice for us poor sinners.

I thank You, dear Jesus,

for having become the priceless Victim

to merit for me the fullness of heavenly favors.

Awaken in me such confidence in You

that their fullness may descend ever more fruitfully upon my soul.

I thank You for offering Yourself in thanksgiving to God

for all His benefits,

spiritual and temporal,

which He has bestowed upon me.

In union with Your offering of Yourself to Your Father

in the Holy Sacrifice of the Mass,

I ask for this special favor:

[State your intention here...]

If it be Your holy Will, grant my request.

Through You I also hope to receive

the grace of perseverance in Your love and faithful service,

a holy death,

and a happy eternity with You in Heaven. Amen.

O Lord, You have given us this Sacred Banquet,

in which Christ is received,

the memory of His Passion is renewed,

the mind is filled with grace,

and a pledge of future glory is given to us.

You have given them bread from Heaven.

Having all sweetness within.

Let us pray.

God our Father,

for Your glory and our salvation

You appointed Jesus Christ eternal High Priest.

May the people He gained for You by His Blood

come to share in the power of His Cross and Resurrection

by celebrating His Memorial in this Eucharist,

for He lives and reigns with You

and the Holy Spirit,

one God, forever.

Amen.

O Jesus, since You have left us a remembrance of Your Passion

beneath the veils of this Sacrament,

grant us, we pray,

so to venerate the sacred mysteries of Your Body and Blood

that we may always enjoy the fruits of Your Redemption,

for You live and reign forever.

Amen.

EFFICACIOUS NOVENA OF THE THREE HAIL MARYS

In Honor of the Power,

Wisdom and Loving Mercy

of the Blessed Virgin Mary

I

Oh, Immaculate Mary,

Virgin most Powerful,

I beseech you,

through that immense Power

which you have received

from the eternal Father,

obtain for me Purity of heart,

Strength to overcome

all the enemies of my soul,

and the special favor

I implore in my present necessity.

(State your intention here...)

Mother most Pure!

Forsake me not,

despise not my prayer,

graciously hear me for God's glory,

your honor, and the welfare of my soul.

To obtain this favor

I honor your Power

by reciting one Hail Mary.

Hail Mary...

II

Oh Virgin Mary,

my Mother,

through that ineffable Wisdom

bestowed upon you by the Incarnate Word of God,

I humbly beseech you,

obtain for me Meekness and Humility of heart,

a perfect knowledge of the divine Will,

and strength to accomplish it always.

Oh Mary, Seat of Wisdom,

as a tender Mother lead me

in the path of Christian Virtue and perfection,

enlighten and enable me

to do what is most pleasing

to your beloved Son,

and obtain my petition.

To obtain this grace

I honor your Wisdom

by reciting one Hail Mary.

Hail Mary...

III

Oh, Mother of Mercy,

Mother of penitent sinners,

I stand before you sinful and sorrowful,

beseeching you through the immense Love

given to you by the Holy Spirit

for us poor sinners,

obtain for me true and perfect contrition for my sins,

which I hate and detest with all my heart,

because I love God.

Mother most Merciful,

help me in my present necessity.

Turn then,

those eyes of Mercy toward us,

Oh Clement,

Oh Loving,

Oh Sweet Virgin Mary!

To obtain this precious gift,

I honor your Loving Mercy

by reciting one Hail Mary.

Hail Mary...

LENTEN NOVENA

Father, all-powerful and ever-living God,

During the Holy Season of Lent

You call us to a closer union with Yourself.

Help me to prepare to celebrate

The Paschal Mystery

With mind and heart renewed.

Give me a spirit of loving reverence

For You, our Father,

And of willing service to my neighbor.

As I recall the great events

That gave us new life in Christ,

Bring the image of Your Son

To perfection within my soul.

This great season of grace is Your gift

To Your family to renew us in spirit.

Give me strength to purify my heart,

To control my desires,

And so to serve You in freedom,

Teach me how to live

In this passing world with my heart set

On the world that will never end.

I ask for the grace

To master my sinfulness

And conquer my pride.

I want to show to those in need

Your goodness to me by being kind to all.

Through my observance of Lent,

Help me to correct my faults

And raise my mind to You,

And thus grow in holiness

That I may deserve

The reward of everlasting life.

In Your mercy grant me this special favor:

(State your intention(s) here...)

The days of the life-giving Death

And glorious Resurrection of Jesus Christ,

Your Son, are approaching.

This is the hour

When He triumphed over Satan's pride,

The time when we celebrate

The great event of our Redemption.

The Suffering and Death of Your Son

Brought life to the whole world,

Moving our hearts to praise Your glory.

The power of the Cross reveals

Your judgment on this world

And the kingship of Christ crucified.

Father, through His love for us

And through His Sufferings, Death and Resurrection,

May I gain eternal life with You in heaven.

MOTHER TERESA EXPRESS NOVENA

An Express Novena is the recitation of 9 Memorares in a row.

THE MEMORARE OF ST. BERNARD

Remember, O most gracious Virgin Mary,

that never was it known

that any one who fled to thy protection,

implored thy help,

and sought thy intercession,

was left unaided.

Inspired with this confidence,

I fly unto thee,

O Virgin of virgins, my Mother,

to thee I come,

before thee I stand sinful and sorrowful.

O Mother of the Word Incarnate!

despise not my petitions,

but, in thy mercy, hear and answer me.

Amen.

NOVENA BEFORE CHRISTMAS

(Begin on December 16 th)

Recite the following prayer every day for 9 days...

Divine Infant,

after the wonders of Your birth in Bethlehem,

You wished to extend Your infinite mercy to the whole world

by calling the Wise Men by heavenly inspiration to Your crib,

which was in this way changed into a royal throne.

You graciously received those holy men

who were obedient to the divine call

and hastened to Your feet.

They recognized and worshiped You as Prince of Peace,

the Redeemer of mankind,

and the very Son of God.

Show us also Your goodness and almighty power.

Enlighten our minds,

strengthen our wills,

and inflame our hearts to know You,

to serve You, and to love You in this life,

that we may merit to find our joy in You

eternally in the life to come.

Jesus, most powerful Child,

I implore You again to help me:

(State your intention here...)

Divine Child,

great omnipotent God,

I implore through Your most Holy Mother's most powerful intercession,

and through the boundless

mercy of Your omnipotence as God,

for a favorable answer to my prayer during this Novena.

Grant me the grace of possessing You eternally

with Mary and Joseph

and of adoring You with Your holy angels and saints.

Amen.

NOVENA FOR CHURCH UNITY

(For 9 Consecutive Days, say the following prayers...)

O Lord Jesus Christ,

who said unto Your Apostles,

"Peace I leave with you,

My peace I give unto you,"

regard not our sins,

but the faith of Your church,

and grant unto her that peace and unity which

are agreeable to Your will,

who live and reign,

God, forever and ever.

Amen.

O Lord, increase in us the faith.

Five Our Father...

Five Hail Mary... and

Five Glory Be...

NOVENA FOR IMPOSSIBLE REQUESTS

(This Novena honours the nine months during which Our Lady carried Our Blessed Lord in her womb.)

"Hail, Holy Queen,

Mother of Mercy,

our life, our sweetness and our hope!

To thee do we cry,

poor banished children of Eve;

to thee do we send up our sighs,

mourning and weeping in this valley of tears.

Turn then, most gracious advocate,

thine eyes of mercy towards us;

and after this our exile,

show unto us the blessed fruit of thy womb Jesus.

O clement, O loving,

O sweet Virgin Mary. Amen."

V - Pray for us, most holy mother of God.

R - That we may be made worthy of the promises of Christ.

"Virgin of the Incarnation,

a thousand times we greet thee,

a thousand times we praise thee

for thy joy when God was incarnated in thee.

Because thou art so powerful

a Virgin and Mother of God,

grant what we ask of thee for the love of God."

Here state your first intention.

Repeat all of above and then state your second intention.

Repeat all of above and then state your third intention.

CONCLUSION:

After the above prayers and intentions, say the Memorare.

Remember, O most Gracious Virgin Mary,

that never was it known

that anyone who fled to thy protection,

implored thy help

or sought thy intercession was left unaided.

Inspired by this confidence,

I fly unto thee,

O Virgin of Virgins,

my mother.

To thee do I cry,

before thee I stand,

sinful and sorrowful.

Mother of the Word Incarnate,

despise not my petitions,

but in thy mercy hear and answer me.

Amen.

Hail Mary...

Blessed and praised be

the Most Holy Sacrament of the Altar,

in Heaven, on earth and everywhere.

AMEN.

NOVENA FOR PENTECOST #1

O Holy Spirit,

who descended upon the Apostles

and filled them with power and wisdom,

watch over me and guide me

in all my thoughts and acts.

Never let me forget to call on you whenever I need help.

Amen.

O Holy Spirit,

Spirit of Truth,

come into our hearts,

shed the brightness of Your light on all nations,

that they may be one in faith and pleasing to You.

NOVENA FOR PENTECOST #2

(9 days leading to Pentecost.)

Holy Spirit, third Person of the Blessed Trinity,

Spirit of truth, love, and holiness,

proceeding from the Father and the Son,

and equal to Them in all things,

I adore You with all my heart.

Holy Spirit, confiding in Your deep,

personal love for me,

I am making this novena for the following request,

if it should be Your holy Will to grant it:

(State Your request here...)

Teach me, Divine Spirit,

to know and seek my last end;

grant me the holy fear of God;

grant me true contrition and patience.

Do not let me fall into sin.

Give me an increase of faith, hope, and charity,

and bring forth in my soul

all the virtues proper to my state of life.

Make me a faithful disciple of Jesus

and an obedient child of the Church.

Give me efficacious grace

sufficient to keep the Commandments

and to receive the Sacraments worthily.

Give me the four Cardinal Virtues,

Your Seven Gifts,

Your Twelve Fruits.

Raise me to perfection in the state of life

to which you have called me

and lead me through a happy death to everlasting life.

I ask this through Christ our Lord.

Holy Spirit, Divine Spirit of light and love,

I consecrate to you my understanding,

heart, and will, my whole being,

for time and for eternity.

May my understanding be always submissive

to Your heavenly inspirations

and to the teaching of the Catholic Church,

of which You are the infallible Guide.

May my heart be ever inflamed with the love of God

and of my neighbor.

May my will be ever conformed to the Divine Will.

May my whole life be faithful

to the imitation of the life and virtues of our Lord and Saviour Jesus Christ,

to Whom with the Father and You

be honor and glory forever.

God, Holy Spirit, Infinite Love of the Father and the Son,

through the pure hands of Mary,

Your Immaculate Spouse,

I place myself this day,

and all the days of my life,

upon Your chosen altar,

the Divine Heart of Jesus,

as a sacrifice to You, consuming fire,

being firmly resolved now more than ever

to hear Your voice

and to do in all things Your most holy and adorable Will.

For the Seven Gifts of the Holy Spirit

Blessed Spirit of Wisdom,

help me to seek God.

Make Him the center of my life and order my life to Him,

so that love and harmony may reign in my soul.

Blessed Spirit of Understanding,

enlighten my mind,

that I may know and love the truths of faith

and make them truly my own.

Blessed Spirit of Counsel,

enlighten and guide me in all my ways,

that I may always know and do Your holy Will.

Make me prudent and courageous.

Blessed Spirit of Fortitude,

uphold my soul in every time of trouble or adversity.

Make me loyal and confident.

Blessed Spirit of Knowledge,

help me to know good from evil.

Teach me to do what is right in the sight of God.

Give me clear vision and firmness in decision.

Blessed Spirit of Piety,

possess my heart,

incline it to a true faith in You,

to a holy love of You, my God,

that with my whole soul I may seek You,

Who are my Father, and find You,

my best, my truest joy.

Blessed Spirit of Holy Fear,

penetrate my inmost heart

that I may ever be mindful of Your presence.

Make me fly from sin,

and give me intense reverence for God

and for my fellow men who are made in God's image.

Prayer

Grant, we beg of You, Almighty God,

that we may so please Your Holy Spirit by our earnest prayers,

that we may, by His grace,

be freed from all temptations and merit

to receive the forgiveness of our sins.

Through Christ our Lord.

Amen.

Say 1 Our Father...

Say 1 Hail Mary... and

Say 1 Glory Be...

Come Holy Spirit, fill the hearts of Thy faithful,

enkindle in them the fire of Thy Love.

Send forth Thy Spirit and they shall be created,

and Thou shalt renew the face of the earth.

Let us pray.

O God, You have taught the hearts of Your faithful people

by sending them the light of Your Holy Spirit.

Grant us by the same Spirit to have a right judgment in all things

and evermore to rejoice in His holy comfort.

Through Christ our Lord.

Amen.

NOVENA FOR POPE FRANCIS

Lord, source of eternal life and truth, give to your shepherd, Francis, a spirit of courage and right judgment, a spirit of knowledge and love. By governing with fidelity those entrusted to his care, may he, as successor to the Apostle Peter and Vicar of Christ, build your Church into a sacrament of unity, love and peace for all the world.

Amen.

V. Let us pray for Francis, the Pope.

R. May the Lord preserve him,

give him a long life,

make him blessed upon the earth,

and not hand him over to the power of his enemies.

V. May your hand be upon your holy servant.

R. And upon your son, whom you have anointed.

Our Father...

Hail Mary...

Glory Be...

NOVENA FOR PRIESTS # 1

Jesus, Good Shepherd,

You sent us the Holy Spirit to guide Your Church

and lead her faithful to You through the ministry of Your priests.

Through the inspiration of the Holy Spirit,

grant to Your priests wisdom in leading,

faithfulness in teaching,

and holiness in guarding Your sacred Mysteries.

As they cry out with all the faithful, "Abba, Father!"

may Your priests be ever more closely identified with You in Your Divine Sonship

and offer their own lives with You,

the one saving Victim.

Make them helpful brothers of one another,

and understanding fathers of all Your people.

On this Pentecost Sunday,

renew in Your priests deeper faith,

greater trust in You,

childlike reliance on our Mother Mary,

and unwavering fidelity to the Holy Father and his bishops.

Holy Mary, intercede for your priests.

St. Joseph, protect them.

St. Michael, defend them.

St. John Vianney, pray for them.

NOVENA FOR PRIESTS # 2

Jesus, meek and humble of heart,

give all priests Thy spirit of humility;

Jesus, poor and worn out for souls,

give all priests Thy spirit of zeal;

Jesus, full of patience and mercy for sinners,

give all priests Thy spirit of compassion;

Jesus, victim for the sins of the world,

give all priests Thy spirit of sacrifice;

Jesus, lover of the little and the poor,

give all priests Thy spirit of charity.

Mary, Queen of the Clergy, pray for us;

and obtain for us numerous and holy priests and religious.

Amen.

NOVENA FOR PRIESTS # 3

O Mary, Mother of Jesus,

you were with Jesus

at the beginning of His life and mission.

You stood beside Jesus when He was lifted on the cross

and gave His life for all.

We ask you now to be with our priests,

who give themselves in service to God's people.

Intercede for them that they may grow in holiness;

proclaim God's word with courage;

celebrate the sacraments with joy;

and be among God's people as Jesus, the Good Shepherd, was.

We offer this prayer to God the Father,

through your intercession,

in the name of your Son, Jesus,

and through the power of the Holy Spirit.

Amen

NOVENA FOR PURIFICATION

(Starts January 24 and ends on February 2.)

O Blessed Mother of God,

who went up to the Temple according to the law

with your offering of little white doves,

pray for me that I too may keep the law

and be pure in heart like you.

Sweet heart of Mary,

be my salvation.

ANNUNCIATION NOVENA #1

I greet you,

Ever-blessed Virgin,

Mother of God,

Throne of Grace,

miracle of Almighty Power!

I greet you,

Sanctuary of the Most Holy Trinity

and Queen of the Universe,

Mother of Mercy

and refuge of sinners!

Most loving Mother,

attracted by your beauty and sweetness,

and by your tender compassion,

I confidently turn to you,

miserable as I am,

and beg of you to obtain for me

from your dear Son

the favor I request in this novena:

(mention your request here).

Obtain for me also,

Queen of heaven,

the most lively contrition for my many sins

and the grace to imitate closely

those virtues which you practiced so faithfully,

especially humility,

purity and obedience.

Above all,

I beg you to be my Mother and Protectress,

to receive me into the number of your devoted children,

and to guide me from your high throne of glory.

Do not reject my petitions,

Mother of Mercy!

Have pity on me,

and do not abandon me during life

or at the moment of my death.

Amen.

ANNUNCIATION NOVENA #2

(Begins March 16 and ends on March 25)

O most holy Virgin Mary,

to whom God sent the Angel Gabriel

to announce that you should be the mother of His Only-Begotten Son,

pray for us who have recourse to you.

Holy, lovely Mary

We give our all to you

What is past and present,

And the future, too.

Blessed be the holy and Immaculate Conception

of the most blessed Virgin Mary, Mother of God.

NOVENA FOR THE DEAD

FIRST DAY

Leader:

Lord our God, receive our supplications, prayers and mortifications and sighs in suffrage for the holy souls for whom we make this novena; and we pray that by the motherly love bestowed on you by your most holy Mother, when she followed you on the way of sorrow up to Mount Calvary, and grant what we ask of you in this novena for your greater honor and glory.

All: AMEN.

Leader: Jesus, through your blood on the cross,

Response (All): Have mercy on the soul of

Leader: Jesus, through the blow you received on your sacred face,

Response (All): Have mercy on the soul of

Leader: Jesus, through the cruel scourging you endured,

Response (All): Have mercy on the soul of

Leader: Jesus, through the crown of thorns that pierced your head,

Response (All): Have mercy on the soul of

Leader: Jesus, through your carrying of the cross,

Response (All): Have mercy on the soul of

Leader: Jesus, through your face covered with blood which you allowed to be imprinted on the veil of Veronica,

Response (All): Have mercy on the soul of

Leader: Jesus, through your garments which were cruelly removed from your wounded body,

Response (All): Have mercy on the soul of

Leader: Jesus, through your holy body nailed on the cross,

Response (All): Have mercy on the soul of

Leader: Jesus, through your side pierced with a lance and from which flowed blood and water.

Response (All): Have mercy on the soul of

SECOND DAY

Leader:

Merciful God, we beseech you, by the pain which your Holy Mother saw you suffer and agonize on the cross, that the holy souls in purgatory be freed from those pains; especially for the soul of _____, for whom we are praying and offering in This novena. Bring those who are submerged in their sins to a true knowledge of their guilt and grant what we ask of you in this novena, for your greater honor and glory.

All: AMEN

Leader: Jesus, through your blood on the cross,

Response (All): Have mercy on the soul of

Leader: Jesus, through the blow you received on your sacred face,

Response (All): Have mercy on the soul of

Leader: Jesus, through the cruel scourging you endured,

Response (All): Have mercy on the soul of

Leader: Jesus, through the crown of thorns that pierced your head,

Response (All): Have mercy on the soul of

Leader: Jesus, through your carrying of the cross,

Response (All): Have mercy on the soul of

Leader: Jesus, through your face covered with blood which you allowed to be imprinted on the veil of Veronica,

Response (All): Have mercy on the soul of

Leader: Jesus, through your garments which were cruelly removed from your wounded body,

Response (All): Have mercy on the soul of

Leader: Jesus, through your holy body nailed on the cross,

Response (All): Have mercy on the soul of

Leader: Jesus, through your side pierced with a lance and from which flowed blood and water.

Response (All): Have mercy on the soul of

THIRD DAY

Leader:

Almighty Father, to whom nobody asks without the hope of receiving, by the intercession of St. Joseph and the Blessed Virgin Mary, enable the suffering souls in purgatory to be able to leave that place, especially for the soul of _____.

We ask this through Christ, our Lord.

All: AMEN.

Leader: Jesus, through your blood on the cross,

Response (All): Have mercy on the soul of

Leader: Jesus, through the blow you received on your sacred face,

Response (All): Have mercy on the soul of

Leader: Jesus, through the cruel scourging you endured,

Response (All): Have mercy on the soul of

Leader: Jesus, through the crown of thorns that pierced your head,

Response (All): Have mercy on the soul of

Leader: Jesus, through your carrying of the cross,

Response (All): Have mercy on the soul of

Leader: Jesus, through your face covered with blood which you allowed to be imprinted on the veil of Veronica,

Response (All): Have mercy on the soul of

Leader: Jesus, through your garments which were cruelly removed from your wounded body,

Response (All): Have mercy on the soul of

Leader: Jesus, through your holy body nailed on the cross,

Response (All): Have mercy on the soul of

Leader: Jesus, through your side pierced with a lance and from which flowed blood and water.

Response (All): Have mercy on the soul of

FOURTH DAY

Leader:

Gracious God,

through whose mercy the saints rest in glory, we beg you to set free those blessed souls in purgatory, especially for the soul of_____, for whom we are praying in this novena. May you radiate your compassion and love to them so they may enter into your Kingdom.

We ask this through Christ, our Lord.

All: AMEN.

Leader: Jesus, through your blood on the cross,

Response (All): Have mercy on the soul of

Leader: Jesus, through the blow you received on your sacred face,

Response (All): Have mercy on the soul of

Leader: Jesus, through the cruel scourging you endured,

Response (All): Have mercy on the soul of

Leader: Jesus, through the crown of thorns that pierced your head,

Response (All): Have mercy on the soul of

Leader: Jesus, through your carrying of the cross,

Response (All): Have mercy on the soul of

Leader: Jesus, through your face covered with blood which you allowed to be imprinted on the veil of Veronica,

Response (All): Have mercy on the soul of

Leader: Jesus, through your garments which were cruelly removed from your wounded body,

Response (All): Have mercy on the soul of

Leader: Jesus, through your holy body nailed on the cross,

Response (All): Have mercy on the soul of

Leader: Jesus, through your side pierced with a lance and from which flowed blood and water.

Response (All): Have mercy on the soul of

FIFTH DAY

Leader:

Sovereign Lord,

in whom it is proper to be merciful, through the intercession of St. Michael, the archangel, and by the sorrow of your Blessed Mother who suffered when the soldier pierced your side with a lance, have mercy on the soul of _____ for whom we are offering this novena and bring him/her to your eternal rest in heaven, for the better glory and honor of your name.

All: AMEN.

Leader: Jesus, through your blood on the cross,

Response (All): Have mercy on the soul of

Leader: Jesus, through the blow you received on your sacred face,

Response (All): Have mercy on the soul of

Leader: Jesus, through the cruel scourging you endured,

Response (All): Have mercy on the soul of

Leader: Jesus, through the crown of thorns that pierced your head,

Response (All): Have mercy on the soul of

Leader: Jesus, through your carrying of the cross,

Response (All): Have mercy on the soul of

Leader: Jesus, through your face covered with blood which you allowed to be imprinted on the veil of Veronica,

Response (All): Have mercy on the soul of

Leader: Jesus, through your garments which were cruelly removed from your wounded body,

Response (All): Have mercy on the soul of

Leader: Jesus, through your holy body nailed on the cross,

Response (All): Have mercy on the soul of

Leader: Jesus, through your side pierced with a lance and from which flowed blood and water.

Response (All): Have mercy on the soul of

SIXTH DAY

Leader:

Lord Jesus Christ,

incline your ears to our petitions. Have mercy on the souls in purgatory, especially for the soul of_____ for whom we make this novena. We humbly ask you to set them free and bring them to the happiness in heaven, for the greater glory and honor of your name.

All: AMEN.

Leader: Jesus, through your blood on the cross,

Response (All): Have mercy on the soul of

Leader: Jesus, through the blow you received on your sacred face,

Response (All): Have mercy on the soul of

Leader: Jesus, through the cruel scourging you endured,

Response (All): Have mercy on the soul of

Leader: Jesus, through the crown of thorns that pierced your head,

Response (All): Have mercy on the soul of

Leader: Jesus, through your carrying of the cross,

Response (All): Have mercy on the soul of

Leader: Jesus, through your face covered with blood which you allowed to be imprinted on the veil of Veronica,

Response (All): Have mercy on the soul of

Leader: Jesus, through your garments which were cruelly removed from your wounded body,

Response (All): Have mercy on the soul of

Leader: Jesus, through your holy body nailed on the cross,

Response (All): Have mercy on the soul of

Leader: Jesus, through your side pierced with a lance and from which flowed blood and water.

Response (All): Have mercy on the soul of

SEVENTH DAY

Leader:

Lord of mercy, hear our prayer.

May our brother/sister _____, whom you called your son/daughter on earth, enter into the Kingdom of peace and light, where your saints live in glory. We ask this through our Lord, Jesus Christ, who lives and reigns with you and Holy Spirit, one God forever and ever.

All: AMEN.

Leader: Jesus, through your blood on the cross,

Response (All): Have mercy on the soul of

Leader: Jesus, through the blow you received on your sacred face,

Response (All): Have mercy on the soul of

Leader: Jesus, through the cruel scourging you endured,

Response (All): Have mercy on the soul of

Leader: Jesus, through the crown of thorns that pierced your head,

Response (All): Have mercy on the soul of

Leader: Jesus, through your carrying of the cross,

Response (All): Have mercy on the soul of

Leader: Jesus, through your face covered with blood which you allowed to be imprinted on the veil of Veronica,

Response (All): Have mercy on the soul of

Leader: Jesus, through your garments which were cruelly removed from your wounded body,

Response (All): Have mercy on the soul of

Leader: Jesus, through your holy body nailed on the cross,

Response (All): Have mercy on the soul of

Leader: Jesus, through your side pierced with a lance and from which flowed blood and water.

Response (All): Have mercy on the soul of

EIGHT DAY

Leader:

Creator and Redeemer of all mankind, through the infinite merits of passion, death and resurrection, we beg you to shower the immense treasures of your clemency on those blessed souls, especially for the eternal repose of the soul of _____. Bring those who are in sin to a true knowledge and repentance and grant what we ask for in this novena, through Christ, our Lord.

All: AMEN.

Leader: Jesus, through your blood on the cross,

Response (All): Have mercy on the soul of

Leader: Jesus, through the blow you received on your sacred face,

Response (All): Have mercy on the soul of

Leader: Jesus, through the cruel scourging you endured,

Response (All): Have mercy on the soul of

Leader: Jesus, through the crown of thorns that pierced your head,

Response (All): Have mercy on the soul of

Leader: Jesus, through your carrying of the cross,

Response (All): Have mercy on the soul of

Leader: Jesus, through your face covered with blood which you allowed to be imprinted on the veil of Veronica,

Response (All): Have mercy on the soul of

Leader: Jesus, through your garments which were cruelly removed from your wounded body,

Response (All): Have mercy on the soul of

Leader: Jesus, through your holy body nailed on the cross,

Response (All): Have mercy on the soul of

Leader: Jesus, through your side pierced with a lance and from which flowed blood and water.

Response (All): Have mercy on the soul of

NINTH DAY

Leader:

Lord God, you are the glory of the believers and the life of the just. Your Son redeemed us by dying and rising to life again. Our brother/sister _____, was faithful and believed in the resurrection. Give to him/her the joys and the blessings of the life to come. We ask this through our Lord Jesus Christ, who lives and reigns with you and the Holy Spirit, one God forever and ever.

All: AMEN.

Leader: Jesus, through your blood on the cross,

Response (All): Have mercy on the soul of

Leader: Jesus, through the blow you received on your sacred face,

Response (All): Have mercy on the soul of

Leader: Jesus, through the cruel scourging you endured,

Response (All): Have mercy on the soul of

Leader: Jesus, through the crown of thorns that pierced your head,

Response (All): Have mercy on the soul of

Leader: Jesus, through your carrying of the cross,

Response (All): Have mercy on the soul of

Leader: Jesus, through your face covered with blood which you allowed to be imprinted on the veil of Veronica,

Response (All): Have mercy on the soul of

Leader: Jesus, through your garments which were cruelly removed from your wounded body,

Response (All): Have mercy on the soul of

Leader: Jesus, through your holy body nailed on the cross,

Response (All): Have mercy on the soul of

Leader: Jesus, through your side pierced with a lance and from which flowed blood and water.

Response (All): Have mercy on the soul of

NOVENA FOR THE ELECTION OF A NEW POPE

Come, Holy Ghost, Creator, come.

From thy bright heavenly throne!

Come, take possession of our souls,

And make them all Thine Own!

Thou who art called the Paraclete,

Best gift of God above,

The Living Spring, The Living Fire,

Sweet Unction, and True Love!

Thou who are sevenfold in Thy grace,

Finger of God's right hand,

His Promise, teaching little ones

To speak and understand!

O guide our minds with thy blest light,

With love our hearts inflame,

And with thy strength, which ne'er decays,

Confirm our mortal frame.

Far from us drive our hellish foe,

True peace unto us bring,

And through all perils guide us safe

Beneath thy sacred wing.

Through Thee may we the Father know,

Through Thee the Eternal Son,

And Thee the Spirit of them both

Thrice blessed Three in One.

Now to the Father, and the Son

Who rose from death, be glory given,

With Thee, O holy Comforter,

Henceforth by all in earth and heaven.

Amen.

Prayer

O Lord, with suppliant humility, we entreat Thee,

that in Thy boundless mercy

Thou wouldst grant the most holy Roman Church a pontiff,

who by his zeal for us,

may be pleasing to Thee,

and by his good government may ever be honored

by Thy people for the glory of Thy name.

Through Our Lord Jesus Christ, Thy Son,

who with Thee livest and reignest world without end.

Amen.

Most Sorrowful and Immaculate Heart of Mary,

pray for us who have recourse to Thee!

NOVENA FOR THE EPIPHANY

While this Novena can be said at any time during the year, it is most popular during the 9 days prior to the Feast of the Epiphany (January), the 9 th day ending on the Feast.

DAY 1

O holy Magi,

you were living in continual expectation

of the rising of the Star of Jacob,

which would announce the birth

of the true Sun of justice,

obtain for us an increase

of faith and charity,

and the grace to live

in continual hope of beholding one day

the light of heavenly glory and eternal joy.

Glory Be...

DAY 2

O holy Magi,

who at the first appearance of the wondrous star

left your native country to go and seek

the newborn king of the Jews,

obtain for us the grace of corresponding

with alacrity to every divine inspiration.

Glory Be...

DAY 3

O holy Magi,

who regarded neither the severity of the season,

nor the inconveniences of the journey,

that you might find the new-born Messiah;

obtain for us the grace

not to allow ourselves to be discouraged

by any of the difficulties which may meet us

in the way of salvation.

Glory Be...

DAY 4

O holy Magi,

who when deserted by the star

in the city of Jerusalem,

sought humbly, and without human respect,

from the rulers of the Church,

the place where you might discover

the object of your journey,

obtain for us the grace to have recourse,

in faith and humility,

in all our doubts and perplexities

to the counsel of our superiors,

who hold the place of God on earth.

Glory Be...

DAY 5

O holy Magi,

who were gladdened by the reappearance

of the star which led you to Bethlehem,

obtain for us from God the grace that,

remaining always faithful to Him in afflictions,

we may be consoled in time by His glory.

Glory Be...

DAY 6

O holy Magi,

who, entering full of faith

into the stable of Bethlehem,

prostrated yourselves on the earth,

to adore the new-born King of the Jews,

though He was surrounded only by signs

of poverty and weakness,

obtain from the Lord for us a lively faith

in the real presence of Jesus

in the Blessed Sacrament,

the true spirit of poverty,

and a Christlike charity

for the poor and suffering.

Glory Be...

DAY 7

O holy Magi,

who offered to Jesus Christ gold, incense, and myrrh,

thereby recognizing Him to be at once King, God, and Man,

obtain from the Lord for us

the grace never to present ourselves

before Him with empty hands,

but that we may continually

offer to Him the gold of charity,

the incense of prayer,

and the myrrh of penance and mortification.

Glory Be...

DAY 8

O holy Magi,

who when warned by an angel

not to return to Herod,

traveled back to your country by another road,

obtain for us from the Lord the grace that,

after having found Him by true repentance,

we may avoid all danger of losing Him again.

Glory Be...

DAY 9

O holy Magi,

who were the first among the Gentiles

called to the knowledge of Jesus Christ,

and who persevered in the faith until your deaths,

obtain for us from the Lord

the grace of living always in conformity

to the baptismal promises

and especially in accordance with our religious vows

(or 'the duties of our state of life'),

leading ever a life of faith,

that like you we may attain to beatific vision

of that God Who now is the object of our faith.

Glory Be...

NOVENA FOR THE HOLY SOULS IN PURGATORY #1

O Jesus, Thou didst suffer and die

that all mankind might be saved

and brought to eternal happiness.

Through the Agony of Thine Crown of Thorns

I offer it to Thy Eternal Father

that Thou wilt hear our pleas

for further mercy on the souls of:

My dear parents and grandparents,

My Jesus, mercy and relief through Thy Sacred Wounds

My brothers and sisters and other near relatives,

My Jesus, mercy and relief through Thy Sacred Wounds

My godparents and sponsors of Confirmation,

My Jesus, mercy and relief through Thy Sacred Wounds

My spiritual and temporal benefactors,

My Jesus, mercy and relief through Thy Sacred Wounds

My friends and neighbors,

My Jesus, mercy and relief through Thy Sacred Wounds

All for whom love or duty bids me pray,

My Jesus, mercy and relief through Thy Sacred Wounds

Those who have offended me,

My Jesus, mercy and relief through Thy Sacred Wounds

Those who have suffered disadvantage of harm through me,

My Jesus, mercy and relief through Thy Sacred Wounds

Those who are especially beloved by Thee,

My Jesus, mercy and relief through Thy Sacred Wounds

Those whose release is near at hand,

My Jesus, mercy and relief through Thy Sacred Wounds

Those who desire most to be united to Thee,

My Jesus, mercy and relief through Thy Sacred Wounds

Those who endure the greatest suffering,

My Jesus, mercy and relief through Thy Sacred Wounds

Those whose release is most remote,

My Jesus, mercy and relief through Thy Sacred Wounds

Those who are least remembered,

My Jesus, mercy and relief through Thy Sacred Wounds

Those who are most deserving on account of their services to the Church,

My Jesus, mercy and relief through Thy Sacred Wounds

The rich who are now the most destitute,

My Jesus, mercy and relief through Thy Sacred Wounds

The mighty who are now powerless,

My Jesus, mercy and relief through Thy Sacred Wounds

The once spiritually blind, who now see their folly,

My Jesus, mercy and relief through Thy Sacred Wounds

The frivolous, who spent their time in idleness,

My Jesus, mercy and relief through Thy Sacred Wounds

The poor, who did not seek the treasures of Heaven,

My Jesus, mercy and relief through Thy Sacred Wounds

The tepid, who devoted little time to prayer,

My Jesus, mercy and relief through Thy Sacred Wounds

The indolent, who neglected to perform good works,

My Jesus, mercy and relief through Thy Sacred Wounds

Those of little faith, who neglected the frequent reception of the Sacraments,

My Jesus, mercy and relief through Thy Sacred Wounds

The habitual sinners, who owe their salvation to a miracle of grace,

My Jesus, mercy and relief through Thy Sacred Wounds

Parents who failed to watch over their children,

My Jesus, mercy and relief through Thy Sacred Wounds

Superiors who were not solicitous

for the salvation of those entrusted to them,

My Jesus, mercy and relief through Thy Sacred Wounds

Those who strove for worldly riches and pleasures,

My Jesus, mercy and relief through Thy Sacred Wounds

The worldly minded, who failed to use their wealth and talents in the service of God,

My Jesus, mercy and relief through Thy Sacred Wounds

Those who witnessed the death of others, but would not think of their own,

My Jesus, mercy and relief through Thy Sacred Wounds

Those who blasphemed and committed sacrilege without due reparation,

My Jesus, mercy and relief through Thy Sacred Wounds

Those who violated the dignity of the human body and mind through impurity,

My Jesus, mercy and relief through Thy Sacred Wounds

Those who are in Purgatory because of me,

My Jesus, mercy and relief through Thy Sacred Wounds

Those who did not provide for the life hereafter,

My Jesus, mercy and relief through Thy Sacred Wounds

Those whose sentence is severe because of the great things entrusted to them, The popes, kings and rulers,

My Jesus, mercy and relief through Thy Sacred Wounds

The bishops and their counselors,

My Jesus, mercy and relief through Thy Sacred Wounds

My teachers and spiritual advisors,

My Jesus, mercy and relief through Thy Sacred Wounds

The deceased priests of this diocese,

My Jesus, mercy and relief through Thy Sacred Wounds

The priests and religious of the Catholic Church,

My Jesus, mercy and relief through Thy Sacred Wounds

The defenders of the holy Catholic Faith,

My Jesus, mercy and relief through Thy Sacred Wounds

Those who die on the battlefield,

My Jesus, mercy and relief through Thy Sacred Wounds

Those who fought for their country,

My Jesus, mercy and relief through Thy Sacred Wounds

Those who were buried in the sea,

My Jesus, mercy and relief through Thy Sacred Wounds

Those who died suddenly, in accidents and from other causes,

My Jesus, mercy and relief through Thy Sacred Wounds

Those who died of sudden illness,

My Jesus, mercy and relief through Thy Sacred Wounds

Those who suffered and died of lingering illnesses,

My Jesus, mercy and relief through Thy Sacred Wounds

Those who died without the last rites of the Church,

My Jesus, mercy and relief through Thy Sacred Wounds

Those who shall die within the next twenty-four hours,

My Jesus, mercy and relief through Thy Sacred Wounds

For those who procured abortions or aborted their children,

My Jesus, mercy and relief through Thy Sacred Wounds

For those who promoted or practiced contraception,

My Jesus, mercy and relief through Thy Sacred Wounds

For those who gave scandal, especially to children,

My Jesus, mercy and relief through Thy Sacred Wounds

My own poor soul when I shall have to appear before Thy judgment seat.

PRAYER

Eternal rest grant unto all of these, O Lord;

and let the perpetual light of Thine countenance

shine upon them soon.

Amen.

NOVENA FOR THE HOLY SOULS IN PURGATORY #2

(By Saint Alphonsus Liguori)

PRAYER TO OUR SUFFERING SAVIOUR FOR THE HOLY SOULS IN PURGATORY

O most sweet Jesus,

through the bloody sweat which Thou didst suffer in the Garden of Gethsemane,

have mercy on these Blessed Souls.

Have mercy on them.

R. Have mercy on them, O Lord.

O most sweet Jesus,

through the pains which Thou didst suffer during Thy most cruel scourging,

have mercy on them.

R. Have mercy on them, O Lord.

O most sweet Jesus,

through the pains which Thou didst suffer in Thy most painful crowning with thorns,

have mercy on them.

R. Have mercy on them, O Lord.

O most sweet Jesus,

through the pains which Thou didst suffer in carrying Thy cross to Calvary,

have mercy on them.

R. Have mercy on them, O Lord.

O most sweet Jesus,

through the pains which Thou didst suffer during Thy most cruel Crucifixion,

have mercy on them.

R. Have mercy on them, O Lord.

O most sweet Jesus,

through the pains which Thou didst suffer in Thy most bitter agony on the Cross,

have mercy on them.

R. Have mercy on them, O Lord.

O most sweet Jesus,

through the immense pain which Thou didst suffer in breathing forth Thy Blessed Soul,

have mercy on them.

R. Have mercy on them, O Lord.

(State your intention(s) here while recommending yourself to the souls in Purgatory.)

Blessed Souls, I have prayed for thee;

I entreat thee, who are so dear to God,

and who are secure of never losing Him,

to pray for me a miserable sinner,

who is in danger of being damned,

and of losing God forever.

Amen.

DAY ONE

Jesus, my Saviour, I have so often deserved to be cast into hell.

 how great would be my suffering if I were now cast away

and obliged to think that I myself had caused my damnation.

I thank Thee for the patience with which Thou hast endured me.

My God, I love Thee above all things

and I am heartily sorry for having offended Thee

because Thou art infinite goodness.

I will rather die than offend Thee again.

Grant me the grace of perseverance.

Have pity on me and at the same time

on those blessed souls suffering in Purgatory.

Mary, Mother of God,

come to their assistance with thy powerful intercession.

Say the following prayers:

1 Our Father...

1 Hail Mary...

The above Prayer to Our Suffering Saviour for the Holy Souls in Purgatory .

DAY TWO

Woe to me, unhappy being,

so many years have I already spent on earth

and have earned naught but hell!

I give Thee thanks, O Lord,

for granting me time even now to atone for my sins.

My good God, I am heartily sorry for having offended Thee.

Send me Thy assistance,

that I may apply the time yet remaining to me

for Thy love and service;

have compassion on me, and,

at the same time,

on the holy souls suffering in Purgatory.

O Mary, Mother of God,

come to their assistance with thy powerful intercession.

Say the following prayers:

1 Our Father...

1 Hail Mary...

The above Prayer to Our Suffering Saviour for the Holy Souls in Purgatory .

DAY THREE

My God! because Thou art infinite goodness,

I love Thee above all things,

and repent with my whole heart of my offenses against Thee.

Grant me the grace of holy perseverance.

Have compassion on me,

and, at the same,

on the holy souls suffering in Purgatory.

And thou, Mary, Mother of God,

come to their assistance with thy powerful intercession.

Say the following prayers:

1 Our Father...

1 Hail Mary...

The above Prayer to Our Suffering Saviour for the Holy Souls in Purgatory .

DAY FOUR

My God! because Thou art infinite goodness,

I am sorry with my whole heart for having offended Thee.

I promise to die rather than ever offend Thee more.

Give me holy perseverance;

have pity on me,

and have pity on those holy souls

that burn in the cleansing fire

and love Thee with all their hearts.

O Mary, Mother of God,

assist them by thy powerful prayers.

Say the following prayers:

1 Our Father...

1 Hail Mary...

The above Prayer to Our Suffering Saviour for the Holy Souls in Purgatory .

DAY FIVE

Woe to me, unhappy being, if Thou, O Lord,

hadst cast me into hell;

for from that dungeon of eternal pain there is no deliverance.

I love Thee above all things,

O infinite God and I am sincerely sorry for having offended Thee again.

Grant me the grace of holy perseverance.

Have compassion on me,

and, at the same time,

on the holy souls suffering in Purgatory.

O Mary, Mother of God,

come to their assistance with thy powerful intercession.

Say the following prayers:

1 Our Father...

1 Hail Mary...

The above Prayer to Our Suffering Saviour for the Holy Souls in Purgatory .

DAY SIX

My Divine Redeemer,

Thou didst die for me on the Cross,

and hast so often united Thyself with me in Holy Communion,

and I have repaid Thee only with ingratitude.

Now, however, I love Thee above all things,

O supreme God;

and I am more grieved at my offenses against Thee than at any other evil.

I will rather die than offend Thee again.

Grant me the grace of holy perseverance.

Have compassion on me, and, at the same time,

on the holy souls suffering in Purgatory.

Mary, Mother of God,

come to their aid with thy powerful intercession.

Say the following prayers:

1 Our Father...

1 Hail Mary...

The above Prayer to Our Suffering Saviour for the Holy Souls in Purgatory .

DAY SEVEN

God, Father of Mercy,

satisfy this their ardent desire!

Send them Thy holy Angel to announce to them that Thou, their Father,

are now reconciled with them through the suffering and death of Jesus,

and that the moment of their deliverance has arrived.

Say the following prayers:

1 Our Father...

1 Hail Mary...

The above Prayer to Our Suffering Saviour for the Holy Souls in Purgatory .

DAY EIGHT

Oh my God! I also am one of these ungrateful beings,

having received so much grace,

and yet despised Thy love and deserved to be cast by Thee into hell.

But Thy infinite goodness has spared me until now.

Therefore, I now love Thee above all things,

and I am heartily sorry for having offended Thee.

I will rather die than ever offend Thee.

Grant me the grace of holy perseverance.

Have compassion on me and,

at the same time,

on the holy souls suffering in Purgatory.

Mary, Mother of God,

come to their aid with thy powerful intercession.

Say the following prayers:

1 Our Father...

1 Hail Mary...

The above Prayer to Our Suffering Saviour for the Holy Souls in Purgatory .

DAY NINE

My God! How was it possible that I,

for so many years, have borne tranquilly the separation from Thee

and Thy holy grace!

O infinite Goodness,

how long-suffering hast Thou shown Thyself to me!

Henceforth, I shall love Thee above all things.

I am deeply sorry for having offended Thee;

I promise rather to die than to again offend Thee.

Grant me the grace of holy perseverance,

and do not permit that I should ever again fall into sin.

Have compassion on the holy souls in Purgatory.

I pray Thee, moderate their sufferings;

shorten the time of their misery;

call them soon unto Thee in heaven,

that they may behold Thee face to face,

and forever love Thee.

Mary, Mother of Mercy,

come to their aid with thy powerful intercession,

and pray for us also who are still in danger of eternal damnation.

Say the following prayers:

1 Our Father...

1 Hail Mary...

The above Prayer to Our Suffering Saviour for the Holy Souls in Purgatory .

NOVENA FOR THE NEEDS OF POPE FRANCIS

God of heaven and earth, Creator of all,

Be always by the side of Your Ambassador Pope Francis.

Guide him in his words and actions,

Sustain him as an instrument of Your peace and compassion,

Give him the wisdom and strength to do Your Will,

Protect him from all evil,

Help him to shepherd the flock of the Church, to bring it to salvation,

And manifest in him Your boundless mercy, Your forgiveness and kindness.

May he always be filled with Your unfathomable love,

And may he be a vessel for that love to fill the world.

Amen.

V. Let us pray for Pope Francis.

R. May the Lord bless him, keep him, and protect him from all harm. May God's spirit shine upon him and give him peace.

Say the following three prayers:

Our Father...

Hail Mary...

Glory Be...

NOVENA FOR THE PROTECTION OF THE UNBORN

O Heavenly Father,

Creator and Giver of all life,

Author of justice,

Source of love and mercy:

Although it is deserving of thine anger and punishment, look with mercy on our nation, which has offended thee by condoning the killing of millions of innocent children, thy precious sons and daughters, who, like all of us, were created in thine image and likeness, but whose only offense was their very existence.

Amen.

O Blessed Lord Jesus Christ, Our Redeemer,

whose inestimable gift of self-sacrificing love

provided the means of Salvation for all mankind

through the shedding of thine innocent blood:

grant that all may come to know thee,

serve thee and love thee,

and thus may know the meaning of true freedom and true liberty,

which never destroys,

but always serves and protects life.

amen.

O Holy Spirit, source of wisdom,

knowledge, understanding, counsel,

fortitude, piety and holy fear:

inspire us with these gifts.

Fill the hearts of the leaders of this nation,

especially those who have the temporal power

and the grave responsibility to make

and interpret and execute laws,

with the desire to do God's will,

to restore justice

and to establish laws

that govern the people of this land

in conformity with the Divine Law,

laws that will preserve,

protect and defend the lives of all sons and daughters of God,

from their earliest beginnings until death.

Amen.

O Mary, Mother of Jesus,

entrusted to be the mother of God's only begotten Son, Our Savior,

through thine obedient consent to God's will,

and who thus became for all people

and all time the model of faith

and of the self-giving love and devotion of Motherhood:

take into thy motherly arms all the babies who are victims of abortion,

that they may receive eternally the comfort of a mother's love.

May thine example and intercession

open the hearts of all who reject God and His holy laws.

comfort all those who suffer remorse because of abortion,

and restore to hope in Christ

those mothers and fathers who grieve

and repent the killing of their children.

Amen.

All Angels and Saints:

may thy guidance and example

show fallen humanity the way to perfect joy

and freedom and peace found only in unity with God

in obedience to His will through salvation in Christ Jesus;

and may thy constant prayers be joined by those

of all the little children,

the "slaughtered innocents"

as a "cloud of witnesses" interceding for sinful man.

Amen.

Glory be to the Father

and to the Son

and to the Holy Spirit.

As it was in the beginning,

is now and ever shall be,

world without end.

Amen.

NOVENA: DAY 1

Say the above prayers,

Psalm 139 (below)

1 Glory Be...

Rosary: The Sorrowful Mysteries

The Magnificat: [Luke 1:46-55] (below)

1 Glory Be...

NOVENA: DAYS 2-9

1 Our Father...

Above prayers

3 Hail Mary...

1 Glory Be...

Psalm 139

Antiphonal (Responsive):

1. O Lord, thou hast searched me, and known me!

2. Thou knowest when I sit down and when I rise up;
   thou discernest my thoughts from afar.

3. Thou searchest out my path and my lying down,
   and art acquainted with all my ways.

4. Even before a word is on my tongue,
   lo, O Lord, thou knowest it altogether.

5. Thou dost beset me behind and before,
   and layest thy hand upon me.

6. Such knowledge is too wonderful for me;
   it is high, I cannot attain it.

7. Whither shall I go from thy Spirit?

Or whither shall I flee from thy presence?

8. If I ascend to heaven, thou art there!

   If I make my bed in Sheol, thou art there!

9. If I take the wings of the morning,

   and dwell in the uttermost parts of the sea;

10. Even there shall thy hand lead me,

    and thy right hand shall hold me.

11. If I say, "Let only darkness cover me,

    and the light about me be night,"

12. Even the darkness is not dark to thee,

    the night is as bright as the day;

    for darkness is as light with thee.

13. For thou didst form my inward parts:

    thou didst knit me together in my mother's womb.

14. I praise thee; for thou art fearful and wonderful.

    Wonderful are thy works! Thou knowest me right well;

15. My frame was not hidden from thee,

    when I was being made in secret,

    intricately wrought in the depths of the earth.

16. Thine eyes beheld my unformed substance;

    in thy book were written, every one of them,

    the days that were formed for me,

    when as yet there was none of them.

17. How precious to me are thy thoughts, O God!

    How vast is the sum of them!

18. If I would count them, they are more than the sand.

    When I awake, I am still with thee.

19. O that thou wouldst slay the wicked, O God,

    and that men of blood would depart from me,

20. Men who maliciously defy thee,

    who lift themselves up against thee for evil!

21. Do I not hate them that hate thee, O Lord?

    And do I not loathe them that rise up against thee?

22. I hate them with perfect hatred;

    I count them my enemies.

23. Search me, O God, and know my heart!

    Try me, and know my thoughts!

24. And see if there be any wicked way in me,

    and lead me in the way everlasting.

Glory be to the Father

and to the Son

and to the Holy Spirit.

As it was in the beginning,

is now and ever shall be,

world without end.

Amen.

The Magnificat: (Luke 1:46-55)

Unison:

My soul doth magnify the Lord

And my spirit hath rejoiced in God my Savior.

For He hath regarded the low estate of

His handmaiden. For behold, from henceforth

all generations will call me blessed;

for He who is mighty hath

done great things for me,

and holy is His name.

And His mercy is on them that fear Him

throughout all generations.

He hath shown strength with His arm;

He hath scattered the proud

in the imagination of their hearts;

He hath put down the mighty

from their thrones,

and exalted the humble and meek;

He hath filled the hungry with good things,

and the rich He hath sent empty away.

He hath helped His servant Israel,

in remembrance of His mercy,

as He spake to our forefathers,

to Abraham and his seed forever.

Glory be to the Father

and to the Son

and to the Holy Spirit.

As it was in the beginning,

is now and ever shall be,

world without end.

Amen.

NOVENA FOR THE SALVATION OF SOULS AND THE CONVERSION OF SINNERS

O JESUS, Thou didst suffer and die

that all mankind might be saved

and brought to eternal happiness.

Through the Agony of Thine Crown of Thorns

I offer it to Thy Eternal Father

that Thou wilt hear our pleas

for further the grace of final perseverance

for the just and mercy on sinners:

My dear parents and grandparents,

My Jesus, pardon and mercy through Thy Sacred Wounds

My brothers and sisters and other near relatives,

My Jesus, pardon and mercy through Thy Sacred Wounds

My godparents and sponsors of Confirmation,

My Jesus, pardon and mercy through Thy Sacred Wounds

My spiritual and temporal benefactors,

My Jesus, pardon and mercy through Thy Sacred Wounds

My friends and neighbors,

My Jesus, pardon and mercy through Thy Sacred Wounds

All for whom love or duty bids me pray,

My Jesus, pardon and mercy through Thy Sacred Wounds

Those who have offended me,

My Jesus, pardon and mercy through Thy Sacred Wounds

Those who will offend me,

My Jesus, pardon and mercy through Thy Sacred Wounds

Those who have suffered disadvantage of harm through me,

My Jesus, pardon and mercy through Thy Sacred Wounds

Those whom I, still a sinner, will offend,

My Jesus, pardon and mercy through Thy Sacred Wounds

Those who are especially beloved by Thee,

My Jesus, pardon and mercy through Thy Sacred Wounds

Those whose death is near at hand,

My Jesus, pardon and mercy through Thy Sacred Wounds

Those who desire most to be united to Thee,

My Jesus, pardon and mercy through Thy Sacred Wounds

Those who endure the greatest sufferings and trials, especially spiritual torments,

My Jesus, pardon and mercy through Thy Sacred Wounds

Those whose death is most remote,

My Jesus, pardon and mercy through Thy Sacred Wounds

Those sinners have no one to pray for them,

My Jesus, pardon and mercy through Thy Sacred Wounds

Those who are most deserving on account of their services to the Church,

My Jesus, pardon and mercy through Thy Sacred Wounds

The rich who do not need Thee and are thus the most destitute,

My Jesus, pardon and mercy through Thy Sacred Wounds

The mighty who spurn Thee,

My Jesus, pardon and mercy through Thy Sacred Wounds

The spiritually blind, that they might see their folly,

My Jesus, pardon and mercy through Thy Sacred Wounds

The frivolous, who spend their time in idleness,

My Jesus, pardon and mercy through Thy Sacred Wounds

The poor, who do not seek the treasures of Heaven,

My Jesus, pardon and mercy through Thy Sacred Wounds

The tepid, who devote little time to prayer,

My Jesus, pardon and mercy through Thy Sacred Wounds

The indolent, who neglect to perform good works,

My Jesus, pardon and mercy through Thy Sacred Wounds

Those of little faith, who neglect the frequent reception of the Sacraments,

My Jesus, pardon and mercy through Thy Sacred Wounds

The habitual sinners, who require for their salvation to a miracle of grace,

My Jesus, pardon and mercy through Thy Sacred Wounds

Parents who fail to watch over their children,

My Jesus, pardon and mercy through Thy Sacred Wounds

Superiors who are not solicitous for the salvation of those entrusted to them,

My Jesus, pardon and mercy through Thy Sacred Wounds

Those who strive for worldly riches and pleasures,

My Jesus, pardon and mercy through Thy Sacred Wounds

The worldly minded, who fail to use their wealth and talents in the service of God,

My Jesus, pardon and mercy through Thy Sacred Wounds

Those who witness the death of others, but do not think of their own,

My Jesus, pardon and mercy through Thy Sacred Wounds

Those who blaspheme and commit sacrilege,

My Jesus, pardon and mercy through Thy Sacred Wounds

Those who violate the dignity of the human body and mind through impurity,

My Jesus, pardon and mercy through Thy Sacred Wounds

Those who sin because of my sins and bad example,

My Jesus, pardon and mercy through Thy Sacred Wounds

Those who do not provide for the life hereafter,

My Jesus, pardon and mercy through Thy Sacred Wounds

Those whose judgment will be severe

because of the great things entrusted to them,

My Jesus, pardon and mercy through Thy Sacred Wounds

The pope, kings and rulers,

My Jesus, pardon and mercy through Thy Sacred Wounds

The bishops and their counselors,

My Jesus, pardon and mercy through Thy Sacred Wounds

My teachers and spiritual advisors,

My Jesus, pardon and mercy through Thy Sacred Wounds

The priests of this diocese,

My Jesus, pardon and mercy through Thy Sacred Wounds

The priests and religious of the Catholic Church,

My Jesus, pardon and mercy through Thy Sacred Wounds

The defenders of the holy Catholic Faith,

My Jesus, pardon and mercy through Thy Sacred Wounds

Those who die on the battlefield,

My Jesus, pardon and mercy through Thy Sacred Wounds

Those who fight for their country,

My Jesus, pardon and mercy through Thy Sacred Wounds

Those who will be buried in the sea,

My Jesus, pardon and mercy through Thy Sacred Wounds

Those who are to die suddenly, in accidents and from other causes,

My Jesus, pardon and mercy through Thy Sacred Wounds

Those who will die of heart attacks,

My Jesus, pardon and mercy through Thy Sacred Wounds

Those who suffer with cancer,

My Jesus, pardon and mercy through Thy Sacred Wounds

Those who suffer with AIDS,

My Jesus, pardon and mercy through Thy Sacred Wounds

Those who shall die without the last rites of the Church,

My Jesus, pardon and mercy through Thy Sacred Wounds

Those who shall die within the next twenty-four hours,
My Jesus, pardon and mercy through Thy Sacred Wounds

For Catholic apostates, heretics, and other unbelievers,
My Jesus, pardon and mercy through Thy Sacred Wounds

For Catholics who hold Masonic membership
or in other secret societies,
My Jesus, pardon and mercy through Thy Sacred Wounds

For the conversion of the Jews, Thy chosen people of old,
My Jesus, pardon and mercy through Thy Sacred Wounds

For abortionists and those who aid them,
My Jesus, pardon and mercy through Thy Sacred Wounds

For women who seek abortions,
My Jesus, pardon and mercy through Thy Sacred Wounds

For those who promote or practice contraception,
My Jesus, pardon and mercy through Thy Sacred Wounds

For those who give scandal, especially to children,

My Jesus, pardon and mercy through Thy Sacred Wounds

My own poor soul when I shall have to appear before Thy judgment seat.

My Jesus, pardon and mercy through Thy Sacred Wounds

PRAYER

Final perseverance and pardon grant unto all of these, O Lord;

and let Thy graces through these petitions

flow unto them and be fruitful.

Amen.

NOVENA IN EXALTATION OF THE HOLY CROSS

Jesus, Who because of Your burning love for us willed to be crucified and to shed Your Most Precious Blood for the redemption and salvation of our souls, look down upon us and grant the petition we ask for

(State your intention here...)

We trust completely in Your Mercy.

Cleanse us from sin by Your Grace, sanctify our work, give us and all those who are dear to us our daily bread, lighten the burden of our sufferings, bless our families, and grant to the nations, so sorely afflicted,

Your Peace, which is the only true peace, so that by obeying Your Commandments we may come at last to the glory of Heaven.

NOVENA IN HONOR OF JESUS AS TRUE KING

[Each day, for 9 days, say the following prayers...]

Pray one Our Father...

Pray one Hail Mary...

Pray one Glory Be...

O Lord our God,

You alone are the Most Holy King and Ruler of All Nations.

We pray to You, Lord,

in the great expectation of receiving from You,

O Divine King,

mercy, peace, justice and all good things.

Protect, O Lord our King,

our families and the land of our birth.

Guard us, we pray,

Most Faithful One!

Protect us from our enemies

and from Your Just Judgment.

Forgive us, O Sovereign King,

our sins against You.

Jesus, You are a King of Mercy.

We have deserved Your Just Judgment.

Have mercy on us,

Lord, and forgive us.

We trust in Your Great Mercy.

O Most Awe-inspiring King,

we bow before You and pray;

may Your reign,

Your kingdom,

be recognized on earth!

Amen.

NOVENA IN HONOR OF MARY HELP OF CHRISTIANS

DAY 1

O Mary, powerful help of those Christians

who approach the throne of your mercy with trust!

Listen to the prayers of your children

who invoke your help to avoid sin and the occasions of sin.

DAY 2

O Mary most holy, kind and merciful mother,

with your visible help you freed the Christian people

from the ferocious assaults of the Muslims.

Free our souls from the attacks of the devil,

the world, and the flesh,

so that we may always overcome the enemies of our salvation.

DAY 3

Most powerful Queen of heaven,

you triumphed over heresies

which sought to tear your children away from the Church.

Come to our assistance so that we may remain steadfast in our faith

and may guard the purity of our hearts

in the midst of the many dangers that beset us.

DAY 4

Mary, our most amiable Mother,

you are the Queen of martyrs

because of the heroic courage and strength you exercised on earth.

Obtain for us the strength we need to be constant in your service

and always to show ourselves your devoted children in life and in death.

DAY 5

Loving Mother Mary,

you showed your powerful protection in the triumph of Pope Pius VII.

Spread your mantle over the Church;

and protect our Shepherd, the Holy Father,

from the attacks of the enemy,

free him from all attacks,

and assist him always as he steers the bark of St. Peter to safety.

DAY 6

Mary, Queen of the Apostles,

take under your protection all the ministers

and the faithful of the Catholic Church.

Fill them with a burning zeal for the salvation of souls,

and give special assistance to missionaries

so that they may succeed to attract all souls to faith in Jesus Christ

and thus form one flock under the guidance of one Shepherd.

DAY 7

Loving and merciful Mother,

you saved Christians from countless misfortunes.

Free us from the plague of infidelity

which seeks to alienate us from the Church and religious observances

by means of corrupt publications

and schools and irreligious sects.

Grant perseverance to the good,

give strength to the weak,

and move sinners to repentance,

so that truth and the Kingdom of Jesus Christ may triumph in the world.

DAY 8

Mary, Pillar of the Church and Help of Christians,

we beg to keep us firmly rooted in our faith

and to protect in us our freedom as children of God.

We promise not to stain our souls with sin

and to obey our Holy Father and the Bishops

in communion with him.

We want to live and die in the bosom of the Church

and to attain eternal salvation.

DAY 9

Most loving Mother Mary,

you have always been the Help of Christians.

Help us with your powerful protection in life

and especially at the hour of our death,

so that, after having loved and venerated you on earth,

we may come to proclaim your mercy in heaven.

PRAYER

Almighty and merciful Lord,

in a marvelous manner you deigned to make the most holy Virgin Mary

a powerful helper in defense of Christians.

Grant that, having fought the good fight under her protection during our life,

we may be victorious over our infernal enemy at the hour of our death.

We make this prayer through Christ our Lord.

Amen.

NOVENA IN HONOR OF SAINT GEORGE

PREPARATORY PRAYER

Almighty and eternal God!

With lively faith

and reverently worshiping Thy divine Majesty,

I prostrate myself before Thee

and invoke with filial trust

Thy supreme bounty and mercy.

Illumine the darkness of my intellect

with a ray of Thy heavenly light

and inflame my heart

with the fire of Thy divine love,

that I may contemplate

the great virtues and merits

of the saint in whose honor

I make this novena,

and following his example

imitate, like him,

the life of Thy divine Son.

Moreover, I beseech Thee

to grant graciously,

through the merits and intercession

of this powerful Helper,

the petition which through him

I humbly place before Thee,

devoutly saving,

"Thy will be done on earth

as it is in heaven."

Vouchsafe graciously to hear it,

if it redounds to Thy greater glory

and to the salvation of my soul.

Amen.

PRAYER IN HONOR OF SAINT GEORGE

O GOD,

who didst grant to Saint George

strength and constancy

in the various torments

which he sustained for our holy faith;

we beseech Thee to preserve,

through his intercession,

our faith from wavering and doubt,

so that we may serve Thee

with a sincere heart faithfully unto death.

Through Christ our Lord.

Amen.

INVOCATION OF SAINT GEORGE

Faithful servant of God

and invincible martyr,

Saint George;

favored by God

with the gift of faith,

and inflamed with an ardent love of Christ,

thou didst fight valiantly

against the dragon of pride,

falsehood, and deceit.

Neither pain nor torture,

sword nor death

could part thee from the love of Christ.

I fervently implore thee

for the sake of this love

to help me by thy intercession

to overcome the temptations

that surround me,

and to bear bravely the trials

that oppress me,

so that I may patiently

carry the cross which is placed upon me;

and let neither distress nor difficulties

separate me from the love of Our Lord Jesus Christ.

Valiant champion of the Faith,

assist me in the combat against evil,

that I may win the crown promised to them

that persevere unto the end.

Prayer

My LORD and my God!

I offer up to Thee

my petition in union

with the bitter passion and death

of Jesus Christ, Thy Son,

together with the merits

of His immaculate and blessed Mother,

Mary ever virgin,

and of all the saints,

particularly with those

of the holy Helper

in whose honor I make this novena.

Look down upon me,

merciful Lord!

Grant me Thy grace and Thy love,

and graciously hear my prayer.

Amen.

NOVENA HONORING THE BODY AND BLOOD OF CHRIST

(Corpus Christi Novena)

I thank You, Jesus, my Divine Redeemer,

for coming upon the earth for our sake,

and for instituting the adorable Sacrament of the Holy Eucharist

in order to remain with us until the end of the world.

I thank You for hiding beneath the Eucharistic species

Your infinite majesty and beauty,

which Your Angels delight to behold,

so that I might have courage to approach the throne of Your Mercy.

I thank You, most loving Jesus,

for having made Yourself my food,

and for uniting me to Yourself with so much love

in this wonderful Sacrament that I may live in You.

I thank You, my Jesus,

for giving Yourself to me in this Blessed Sacrament,

and so enriching it with the treasures of Your love

that You have no greater gift to give me.

I thank You not only for becoming my food

but also for offering Yourself as a continual sacrifice

to Your Eternal Father for my salvation.

I thank You, Divine Priest,

for offering Yourself as a Sacrifice daily upon our altars

in adoration and homage to the Most Blessed Trinity,

and for making amends for our poor and miserable adorations.

I thank You for renewing in this daily Sacrifice

the actual Sacrifice of the Cross offered on Calvary,

in which You satisfy Divine justice for us poor sinners.

I thank You, dear Jesus,

for having become the priceless Victim to merit for me

the fullness of heavenly favors.

Awaken in me such confidence in You

that their fullness may descend ever more fruitfully upon my soul.

I thank You for offering Yourself

in thanksgiving to God for all His benefits,

spiritual and temporal,

which He has bestowed upon me.

In union with Your offering of Yourself to Your Father

in the Holy Sacrifice of the Mass,

I ask for this special favor:

(Mention your intentions here...)

If it be Your holy Will,

grant my request.

Through You I also hope to receive

the grace of perseverance in Your love and faithful service,

a holy death, and a happy eternity with You in Heaven.

Amen.

O Lord, You have given us this Sacred Banquet,

in which Christ is received,

the memory of His Passion is renewed,

the mind is filled with grace,

and a pledge of future glory is given to us.

You have given them bread from Heaven.

Having all sweetness within.

Let us pray. God our Father,

for Your glory and our salvation

You appointed Jesus Christ eternal High Priest.

May the people He gained for You by His Blood

come to share in the power of His Cross and Resurrection

by celebrating His Memorial in this Eucharist,

for He lives and reigns with You and the Holy Spirit,

one God, forever.

Amen.

O Jesus, since You have left us a remembrance of Your Passion

beneath the veils of this Sacrament,

grant us, we pray,

so to venerate the sacred mysteries of Your Body and Blood

that we may always enjoy the fruits of Your Redemption,

for You live and reign forever.

Amen.

NOVENA TO THE IMMACULATE CONCEPTION #1

(To commemorate the Immaculate Conception)

First, recite the Prayer to the Immaculate Conception.

PRAYER TO THE IMMACULATE CONCEPTION

O God,

who by the Immaculate Conception

of the Blessed Virgin Mary,

did prepare a worthy dwelling place for Your Son,

we beseech You that,

as by the foreseen death of this, Your Son,

You did preserve Her from all stain,

so too You would permit us,

purified through Her intercession,

to come unto You.

Through the same Lord Jesus Christ,

Your Son, who lives and reigns with You

in the unity of the Holy Spirit,

God, world without end.

Amen.

Then, recite the appropriate prayer of each of the 9 days...

DAY ONE

O most Holy Virgin,

who was pleasing to the Lord and became His mother,

immaculate in body and spirit,

in faith and in love,

look kindly on me as I implore your powerful intercession.

O most Holy Mother,

who by your blessed Immaculate Conception,

from the first moment of your conception

did crush the head of the enemy,

receive our prayers as we implore you

to present at the throne of God the favor we now request...

(State your intention here...)

O Mary of the Immaculate Conception,

Mother of Christ,

you had influence with your Divine Son while upon this earth;

you have the same influence now in heaven.

Pray for us

and obtain for us from him

the granting of my petition if it be the Divine Will.

Amen.

DAY TWO

O Mary, ever blessed Virgin,

Mother of God,

Queen of angels and of saints,

we salute you with the most profound veneration

and filial devotion

as we contemplate your holy Immaculate Conception,

We thank you for your maternal protection

and for the many blessings that we have received

through your wondrous mercy

and most powerful intercession.

In all our necessities

we have recourse to you

with unbounded confidence.

O Mother of Mercy,

we beseech you now to hear our prayer

and to obtain for us of your Divine Son

the favor that we so earnestly request in this novena...

(State your intention here...)

O Mary of the Immaculate Conception,

Mother of Christ,

you had influence with your Divine Son while upon this earth;

you have the same influence now in heaven.

Pray for us

and obtain for us from him

the granting of my petition if it be the Divine Will.

Amen.

DAY THREE

O Blessed Virgin Mary,

glory of the Christian people,

joy of the universal Church

and Mother of Our Lord,

speak for us to the Heart of Jesus,

who is your Son and our brother.

O Mary, who by your holy Immaculate Conception

did enter the world free from stain,

in your mercy obtain for us from Jesus

the special favor which we now so earnestly seek...

(State your intention here...)

O Mary of the Immaculate Conception,

Mother of Christ,

you had influence with your Divine Son while upon this earth;

you have the same influence now in heaven.

Pray for us

and obtain for us from him

the granting of my petition if it be the Divine Will.

Amen.

DAY FOUR

O Mary, Mother of God,

endowed in your glorious Immaculate Conception

with the fullness of grace;

unique among women

in that you are both mother and virgin;

Mother of Christ and Virgin of Christ,

we ask you to look down with a tender heart

from your throne and listen to our prayers

as we earnestly ask that you obtain for us

the favor for which we now plead...

(State your intention here...)

O Mary of the Immaculate Conception,

Mother of Christ,

you had influence with your Divine Son while upon this earth;

you have the same influence now in heaven.

Pray for us

and obtain for us from him

the granting of my petition if it be the Divine Will.

Amen.

DAY FIVE

O Lord, who, by the Immaculate Conception of the Virgin Mary,

did prepare a fitting dwelling for your Son,

we beseech you that as by the foreseen death of your Son,

you did preserve her from all stain of sin,

grant that through her intercession,

we may be favored with the granting of the grace

that we seek for at this time...

(State your intention here...)

O Mary of the Immaculate Conception,

Mother of Christ,

you had influence with your Divine Son while upon this earth;

you have the same influence now in heaven.

Pray for us

and obtain for us from him

the granting of my petition if it be the Divine Will.

Amen.

DAY SIX

Glorious and immortal Queen of Heaven,

we profess our firm belief in your Immaculate Conception

preordained for you in the merits of your Divine Son.

We rejoice with you in your Immaculate Conception.

To the one ever-reigning God,

Father, Son, and Holy Spirit,

three in one Person,

one in nature,

we offer thanks for your blessed Immaculate Conception.

O Mother of the Word mad Flesh,

listen to our petition as we ask

this special grace during this novena...

(State your intention here...)

O Mary of the Immaculate Conception,

Mother of Christ,

you had influence with your Divine Son while upon this earth;

you have the same influence now in heaven.

Pray for us

and obtain for us from him

the granting of my petition if it be the Divine Will.

Amen.

DAY SEVEN

O Immaculate Virgin, Mother of God, and my mother,

from the sublime heights of your dignity

turn your merciful eyes upon me while I,

full of confidence in your bounty

and keeping in mind your Immaculate conception

and fully conscious of your power,

beg of you to come to our aid

and ask your Divine Son to grant the favor

we earnestly seek in this novena,

if it be beneficial for our immortal souls

and the souls for whom we pray.

Amen.

(State your intention here...)

O Mary of the Immaculate Conception,

Mother of Christ,

you had influence with your Divine Son while upon this earth;

you have the same influence now in heaven.

Pray for us

and obtain for us from him

the granting of my petition if it be the Divine Will.

DAY EIGHT

O Most gracious Virgin Mary,

beloved Mother of Jesus Christ, our Redeemer,

intercede with him for us

that we be granted the favor which we petition

for so earnestly in this novena...

(State your intention here...)

O Mother of the Word Incarnate,

we feel animated with confidence

that your prayers in our behalf

will be graciously heard before the throne of God.

O Glorious Mother of God,

in memory of your joyous Immaculate Conception,

hear our prayers and obtain for us our petitions.

O Mary of the Immaculate Conception,

Mother of Christ,

you had influence with your Divine Son while upon this earth;

you have the same influence now in heaven.

Pray for us

and obtain for us from him

the granting of my petition if it be the Divine Will.

Amen.

DAY NINE

O Mother of the King of the Universe,

most perfect member of the human race,

"our tainted nature's solitary boast,"

we turn to you as mother,

advocate, and mediatrix. O Holy Mary,

assist us in our present necessity.

By your Immaculate Conception,

O Mary conceived without sin,

we humbly beseech you from the bottom of our heart

to intercede for us with your Divine Son

and ask that we be granted the favor for which we now plead...

(State your intention here...)

O Mary of the Immaculate Conception,

Mother of Christ,

you had influence with your Divine Son while upon this earth;

you have the same influence now in heaven.

Pray for us

and obtain for us from him

the granting of my petition if it be the Divine Will.

Amen.

On the last day of this Novena, recite the Litany of the Blessed Virgin.

LITANY OF THE BLESSED VIRGIN MARY

Lord, have mercy on us

Christ, have mercy on us

Lord, have mercy on us

Christ, hear us

Christ, graciously hear us

God the Father of heaven, have mercy on us

God the Son, Redeemer of the World, have mercy on us

God the Holy Spirit, ...

Holy Trinity, one God, ...

Holy Mary, pray for us

Holy Mother of God, pray for us

Holy Virgin of virgins, ...

Mother of Christ, ...

Mother of Divine Grace, ...

Mother most pure, ...

Mother most chaste, ...

Mother inviolate, ...

Mother undefiled, ...

Mother most amiable, ...

Mother most admirable, ...

Mother of good counsel, ...

Mother of our Creator, ...

Mother of our Saviour, ...

Virgin most prudent, ...

Virgin most venerable, ...

Virgin most renowned, ...

Virgin most powerful, ...

Virgin most merciful, ...

Virgin most faithful, ...

Mirror of justice, ...

Seat of wisdom, ...

Cause of our joy, ...

Spiritual vessel, ...

Vessel of honor, ...

Singular vessel of devotion, ...

Mystical rose, ...

Tower of David, ...

Tower of ivory, ...

House of gold, ...

Ark of the covenant, ...

Gate of heaven, ...

Morning star, ...

Health of the sick, ...

Refuge of sinners, ...

Comforter of the afflicted, ...

Help of Christians, ...

Queen of Angels, ...

Queen of Patriarchs, ...

Queen of Prophets, ...

Queen of Apostles, ...

Queen of Martyrs, ...

Queen of Confessors, ...

Queen of Virgins, ...

Queen of all Saints, ...

Queen conceived without original sin, ...

Queen assumed into heaven, ...

Queen of the most holy Rosary, ...

Queen of Peace, ...

Lamb of God, who takes away the sins of the world, spare us, O Lord

Lamb of God, who takes away the sins of the world, graciously hear us, O Lord

Lamb of God, who takes away the sins of the world, have mercy on us.

Grant we beseech Thee, O Lord God,

that we, Thy servants,

may enjoy perpetual health of mind and body:

and, by the glorious intercession of the blessed Mary, ever Virgin,

be delivered from present sorrow and enjoy eternal gladness.

Through Christ, our Lord.

Amen.

NOVENA TO THE IMMACULATE CONCEPTION #2

O Mary Immaculate!

Guard with loving care this country dedicated to thee.

Let thy purity keep it pure.

Watch over its institutions.

As thou art the Refuge of all sinners,

this country is the refuge of the exiled and the oppressed.

Guide it ever in the ways of peace.

Let not its prosperity be its ruin.

Alas! Many of its children,

who know not what they do,

are walking in uncertain paths,

which are dark, and lead them away from the truth.

Mother of all, pray for us and plead for them,

that we, thy children,

may love and adore thy adorable Son with more fervent faith,

and that those who are wandering in error's path may,

through thy intercession,

return to the one Fold of the True Shepard,

to thy Son, our Saviour, Jesus Christ.

Amen.

NOVENA TO THE IMMACULATE CONCEPTION #3

O God,

who by the Immaculate Conception of the Blessed Virgin Mary,

did prepare a worthy dwelling place for Your Son,

we beseech You that,

as by the foreseen death of this, Your Son,

You did preserve Her from all stain,

so too You would permit us,

purified through Her intercession,

to come unto You.

Through the same Lord Jesus Christ, Your Son,

who lives and reigns with You in the unity of the Holy Spirit,

God, world without end.

Amen.

DAY ONE

O most Holy Virgin,

who was pleasing to the Lord and became His mother,

immaculate in body and spirit,

in faith and in love,

look kindly on me as I implore your powerful intercession.

O most Holy Mother,

who by your blessed Immaculate Conception,

from the first moment of your conception

did crush the head of the enemy,

receive our prayers as we implore you

to present at the throne of God the favor we now request...

[Mention your intention(s) here...]

O Mary of the Immaculate Conception, Mother of Christ,

you had influence with your Divine Son while upon this earth;

you have the same influence now in heaven.

Pray for us and obtain for us from Him

the granting of my petition if it be the Divine Will.

Amen.

DAY TWO

O Mary, ever blessed Virgin, Mother of God,

Queen of angels and of saints,

we salute you with the most profound veneration and filial devotion

as we contemplate your holy Immaculate Conception,

We thank you for your maternal protection

and for the many blessings

that we have received through your wondrous mercy

and most powerful intercession.

In all our necessities we have recourse to you with unbounded confidence.

O Mother of Mercy,

we beseech you now to hear our prayer

and to obtain for us of your Divine Son

the favor that we so earnestly request in this novena...

[Mention your intention(s) here...]

O Mary of the Immaculate Conception, Mother of Christ,

you had influence with your Divine Son while upon this earth;

you have the same influence now in heaven.

Pray for us and obtain for us from Him

the granting of my petition if it be the Divine Will.

Amen.

DAY THREE

O Blessed Virgin Mary,

glory of the Christian people,

joy of the universal Church and Mother of Our Lord,

speak for us to the Heart of Jesus,

who is your Son and our brother.

O Mary, who by your holy Immaculate Conception

did enter the world free from stain,

in your mercy obtain for us from Jesus

the special favor which we now so earnestly seek...

[Mention your intention(s) here...]

O Mary of the Immaculate Conception, Mother of Christ,

you had influence with your Divine Son while upon this earth;

you have the same influence now in heaven.

Pray for us and obtain for us from Him

the granting of my petition if it be the Divine Will.

Amen.

DAY FOUR

O Mary, Mother of God,

endowed in your glorious Immaculate Conception

with the fullness of grace;

unique among women in that you are both mother and virgin;

Mother of Christ and Virgin of Christ,

we ask you to look down with a tender heart from your throne

and listen to our prayers

as we earnestly ask that you obtain for us

the favor for which we now plead...

[Mention your intention(s) here...]

O Mary of the Immaculate Conception, Mother of Christ,

you had influence with your Divine Son while upon this earth;

you have the same influence now in heaven.

Pray for us and obtain for us from Him

the granting of my petition if it be the Divine Will.

Amen.

DAY FIVE

O Lord, who, by the Immaculate Conception of the Virgin Mary,

did prepare a fitting dwelling for your Son,

we beseech You that as by the foreseen death of Your Son,

You did preserve her from all stain of sin,

grant that through her intercession,

we may be favored with the granting of the grace

that we seek for at this time...

[Mention your intention(s) here...]

O Mary of the Immaculate Conception, Mother of Christ,

you had influence with your Divine Son while upon this earth;

you have the same influence now in heaven.

Pray for us and obtain for us from Him

the granting of my petition if it be the Divine Will.

Amen.

DAY SIX

Glorious and immortal Queen of Heaven,

we profess our firm belief in your Immaculate Conception

preordained for you in the merits of your Divine Son.

We rejoice with you in your Immaculate Conception.

To the one ever-reigning God,

Father, Son, and Holy Spirit,

three in one Person,

one in nature,

we offer thanks for your blessed Immaculate Conception.

O Mother of the Word mad Flesh,

listen to our petition

as we ask this special grace during this novena...

[Mention your intention(s) here...]

O Mary of the Immaculate Conception, Mother of Christ,

you had influence with your Divine Son while upon this earth;

you have the same influence now in heaven.

Pray for us and obtain for us from Him

the granting of my petition if it be the Divine Will.

Amen.

DAY SEVEN

O Immaculate Virgin, Mother of God, and my mother,

from the sublime heights of your dignity

turn your merciful eyes upon me while I,

full of confidence in your bounty

and keeping in mind your Immaculate conception

and fully conscious of your power,

beg of you to come to our aid

and ask your Divine Son

to grant the favor we earnestly seek in this novena...

if it be beneficial for our immortal souls

and the souls for whom we pray.

[Mention your intention(s) here...]

O Mary of the Immaculate Conception, Mother of Christ,

you had influence with your Divine Son while upon this earth;

you have the same influence now in heaven.

Pray for us and obtain for us from Him

the granting of my petition if it be the Divine Will.

Amen.

DAY EIGHT

O Most gracious Virgin Mary,

beloved Mother of Jesus Christ, our Redeemer,

intercede with Him for us

that we be granted the favor

which we petition for so earnestly in this novena...

O Mother of the Word Incarnate,

we feel animated with confidence that your prayers

in our behalf will be graciously heard

before the throne of God.

O Glorious Mother of God,

in memory of your joyous Immaculate Conception,

hear our prayers and obtain for us our petitions.

[Mention your intention(s) here...]

O Mary of the Immaculate Conception, Mother of Christ,

you had influence with your Divine Son while upon this earth;

you have the same influence now in heaven.

Pray for us and obtain for us from Him

the granting of my petition if it be the Divine Will.

Amen.

DAY NINE

O Mother of the King of the Universe,

most perfect member of the human race,

"our tainted nature's solitary boast,"

we turn to you as mother,

advocate, and mediatrix.

O Holy Mary, assist us in our present necessity.

By your Immaculate Conception,

O Mary conceived without sin,

we humbly beseech you from the bottom of our heart

to intercede for us with your Divine Son

and ask that we be granted the favor

for which we now plead...

[Mention your intention(s) here...]

O Mary of the Immaculate Conception, Mother of Christ,

you had influence with your Divine Son while upon this earth;

you have the same influence now in heaven.

Pray for us and obtain for us from Him

the granting of my petition if it be the Divine Will.

Amen.

NOVENA TO THE IMMACULATE CONCEPTION #4

O Mary Immaculate, lily of purity, I salute you,

because from the very first instant of your conception

you were filled with grace.

I thank and adore the Most Holy Trinity

for having imparted to you favors so sublime.

O Mary, full of grace,

help me to share,

even though just a little,

in the fullness of grace so wonderfully bestowed on you

in your Immaculate Conception.

With firm confidence in your never failing intercession,

we beseech you to obtain for us the intention of this novena,

[State your intention here...]

and also that purity of mind, heart,

and body necessary to unite us with God.

Amen.

O Mary, conceived without sin,

pray for us who have recourse to you.

O Mother of God, by your Immaculate Conception,

intercede for us with your Divine Son,

and obtain for us from Him,

the favor for which we pray.

Amen.

A NOVENA IN HONOR OF THE NAME OF JESUS

O merciful Jesus!

Who didst in Thine early infancy

commence Thine office of Saviour,

by shedding Thy precious Blood,

and assuming for us that Name which is above all names;

we thank Thee for such early proofs of Thine infinite love;

we venerate Thy sacred Name,

in union with the profound respect of the Angel

who first announced it to the earth,

and unite our affections to the sentiments of tender devotion

which the adorable Name of Jesus has in all ages

enkindled in the hearts of Thy servants.

Animated with a firm faith in Thine unerring word,

and penetrated with confidence in Thy mercy,

we now most humbly remind Thee of the promise Thou hast made,

that when two or three should assemble in Thy Name,

Thou Thyself wouldst be in the midst of them.

Come, then, into the midst of us,

most amiable Jesus!

for it is in Thy Sacred Name we are here assembled.

Come into our hearts,

that Thy Holy Spirit may pray in and by us;

and mercifully grant us,

through that adorable Name,

which is the joy of heaven,

the terror of hell,

the consolation of the afflicted,

and the solid ground of our unlimited confidence,

all the petitions we make in this Novena.

O Blessed Mother of our Redeemer;

who didst participate so deeply

in the sufferings of thy dear Son,

when He shed His sacred Blood,

and assumed for us the Name of Jesus;

obtain for us through that adorable Name,

the favors we petition in this Novena.

Beg, also, that the most ardent love

may imprint on our hearts that sacred Name,

that it may be always in our minds,

and frequently on our lips;

that it may be our defense in temptations,

and our refuge in danger,

during our lives,

and our consolation and support

in the hour of death.

Amen.

NOVENA IN HONOR OF THE NATIVITY AND INFANCY OF OUR LORD

I

Eternal Father,

I offer to Thine honor and glory,

for my eternal salvation

and for the salvation of the whole world,

the mystery of the birth of our divine Redeemer.

Glory be...

II.

Eternal Father,

I offer to Thine honor and glory,

for my eternal salvation

and for the salvation of the whole world,

the sufferings of the most holy Virgin and Saint Joseph

on that long and weary journey from Nazareth to Bethlehem,

and the anguish of their hearts

at not finding a place of shelter

when the Saviour of the world was about to be born.

Glory be...

III.

Eternal Father,

I offer to Thine honor and glory,

for my eternal salvation

and for the salvation of the whole world,

the sufferings of Jesus in the manger where He was born,

the cold He suffered,

the tears He shed and His tender infant cries.

Glory be...

IV.

Eternal Father,

I offer to Thine honor and glory,

for my eternal salvation

and for the salvation of the whole world,

the pain which the Divine Child Jesus felt in His tender Body,

when He submitted to the rite of circumcision:

I offer Thee that Precious Blood

which He then first shed for the salvation of all mankind.

Glory be...

V.

Eternal Father,

I offer to Thine honor and glory,

for my eternal salvation

and for the salvation of the whole world,

the humility, mortification, patience, charity

and all the virtues of the Child Jesus;

I thank Thee, I love Thee,

and I bless Thee infinitely

for this ineffable mystery of the Incarnation of the Word of God.

Glory be...

V. The Word was made flesh;

R. And dwelt amongst us.

Let us pray.

O God, whose only-begotten Son

hath appeared in the substance of our flesh;

grant, we beseech Thee,

that through Him,

whom we acknowledge to have been outwardly like unto us,

we may deserve to be renewed in our inward selves.

Who liveth and reigneth with Thee for ever and ever.

Amen.

NOVENA IN REPARATION FOR OFFENSES AGAINST LIFE.

Say the following prayers for 9 days in a row.

AN ACT OF REPARATION

Sacred Heart of Jesus,

we offer you an act of reparation

for the indifference often shown to you.

We ourselves have been inattentive many times.

Not only do we now ask your pardon

but we also declare our readiness

to atone both for our personal offenses

and for the faults of others.

We are resolved to expiate every outrage committed against you.

We wish to make amends too

for the injustices perpetrated against the poor and unprotected.

In reparation for all violations of your Divine honor

and of the rights of our fellowmen,

we offer the satisfaction you once made

to your Eternal Father on the cross

and which you continue to renew daily on our altars.

In union with the faithful on earth,

we promise to make recompense, as far as we can,

for all neglect of your great love

and for the sins we and others have committed.

Loving Jesus, through the intercession of the Blessed Virgin Mary,

deign to receive our act of reparation

and keep us faithful to you,

so that we may one day come to that home

where you live and reign with the Father and the Holy Spirit,

one God, for ever and ever.

Amen.

ACT OF CONSECRATION

Jesus, Redeemer of the human race,

we freely consecrate ourselves today to your Most Sacred Heart.

We grieve that many do not yet know you;

many, too, reject you.

Have mercy on them all, most merciful Jesus,

and draw them to your Sacred Heart.

We pray that you, O Lord,

will be King not only of the faithful

who have never forsaken you,

but also of the prodigals.

Grant that all may be admitted to your Father's house.

We pray, too, that you will be King

of those who are now deceived by erroneous opinions,

or whom discord keeps unmindful of you.

Call them to believe in you

so that soon there may be but one flock and one Shepherd.

Grant, O Lord, to all your people,

assurance of freedom and immunity from harm;

give tranquility to all nations;

make the world resound from pole to pole with one cry:

Praise to the Divine Heart

that made possible our salvation;

to it be glory and honor for ever.

Amen.

MIRACULOUS 54 DAYS ROSARY NOVENA

Church history reveals to us that on March 3, 1884, Our Lady of Pompeii appeared before the gravely ill daughter of an Italian military officer. Through her, Our Lady gave the world the miraculous devotion of the 54 days Rosary Novena.

For over a year, Fortuna Agrelli had been in great distress even near death. So serious was her illness that her case had been given-up as hopeless by the most celebrated physicians. In desperation, on February 16 th, the afflicted girl and her family began a novena of Rosaries.

One evening two weeks later, the Queen of the Holy Rosary appeared to Fortuna. Sitting upon a high throne, surrounded by luminous figures, Our Lady was holding the Divine Child on her lap and a Rosary in her hand. Both were arrayed in golden garments and were accompanied by Sts.

Dominic and Catherine of Siena.

Our Lady said, "Child, your faith has pleased me. Whoever desires to obtain favors from me should make three Novenas of the prayers of the Rosary, and three Novenas in thanksgiving."

Obedient to Our Lady's invitation, Fortuna and her family completed the six novenas whereupon the young girl was restored to perfect health and her family showered with many blessings.

THE DEVOTION OF THE MIRACULOUS ROSARY NOVENA

To complete one Novena, a person must say the Rosary for 9 days. Three Novenas of 9 days must be said to obtain the favor. Then, three more Novenas must be said in Thanksgiving. In total, there must be 27 days of Rosary prayers to obtain the favor and 27 days of Rosary prayers in Thanksgiving. This makes a total of 54 days.

Whether the prayer intention has been received or not after the first 27 days (3 Novenas), the person must still say the 3 Rosary prayer Novenas (27 days) in Thanksgiving.

From day to day, the meditations are in accordance with the guideline followed in the Catholic Church. These included the Joyful Mysteries, the Sorrowful Mysteries, and the Glorious Mysteries. The "Mysteries of Light" (aka the "Luminous Mysteries") are not said normally.

NOVENA OF CONFIDENCE TO THE SACRED HEART

O Lord Jesus Christ,

To your most Sacred Heart,

I confide this/these intention(s):

(State you intention(s) here...)

Only look upon me,

And then do

What your Sacred Heart inspires.

Let your Sacred Heart decide

I count on it

I trust in it

I throw myself on Your mercy,

Lord Jesus!

You will not fail me.

Sacred Heart of Jesus,

I trust in You.

Sacred Heart of Jesus,

I believe in Your love for me.

Sacred Heart of Jesus,

Your Kingdom come.

O Sacred Heart of Jesus,

I have asked you for many favors,

But I earnestly implore this one.

Take it.

Place it in Your open, broken Heart;

And, when the Eternal Father looks upon It,

Covered with Your Precious Blood,

He will not refuse it.

It will be no longer my prayer,

But Yours, O Jesus.

O Sacred Heart of Jesus,

I place all my trust in You.

Let me not be disappointed.

Amen.

NOVENA OF GRACE

(March 4 to 12)

PREPARATORY PRAYERS

Priest:

In the Name of the Father,

and of the Son,

and of the Holy Ghost.

Amen.

O Jesus, answer our petitions as we kneel before Thee.

People:

O Heart of Jesus,

hear and grant our prayers.

Priest:

Pray for us,

Saint Francis Xavier,

People:

that we may be made worthy of the promises of Christ.

Priest:

Let us pray:

Come, Holy Ghost,

fill the hearts of Thy faithful.

Enkindle in them the fire of Thy love.

Send forth Thy spirit

and they shall be created,

People:

and Thou shalt renew the face of the earth.

Priest:

Glory be to the Father,

and to the Son,

and to the Holy Ghost,

People:

as it was in the beginning,

is now,

and ever shall be,

world without end.

Amen.

All together:

O most lovable

and loving Saint Francis Xavier

in union with thee

I adore the Divine Majesty.

The remembrance of the favors

with which God blessed thee during life

and of thy glory after death

fills me with joy;

and I unite with thee

in offering to Him

my humble tribute

of thanksgiving and of praise.

I implore thee to secure for me

through thy powerful intercession

the inestimable blessing

of living and dying

in the state of grace.

I also beseech thee

to obtain for me

the favor I ask in this novena.

(State your intentions here...)

But if what I ask

is not for the glory of God

and for the good of my soul

do thou obtain for me

what is more conducive to both.

Amen.

Our Father...

Hail Mary...

Glory Be...

Priest:

Pray for us,

Saint Francis Xavier,

People:

That we may be made worthy of the promises of Christ.

HYMN TO SAINT FRANCIS XAVIER

Oh, Father Saint Francis, we kneel at thy feet,

While blessings and favors we beg and entreat,

That thou from thy bright throne in heaven above

Wouldst look on thy clients with pity and love.

Saint Francis Xavier, Oh pray for us!

Saint Francis Xavier, Oh pray for us!

Oh, Father Saint Francis, thy words were once strong

Against Satan's wiles and an infidel throng.

Not less is thy might where in heaven thou art;

Oh, come to our aid, in our battle take part.

Saint Francis Xavier, Oh pray for us!

Saint Francis Xavier, Oh pray for us!

ST. FRANCIS XAVIER'S PRAYER FOR UNBELIEVERS

All together:

Eternal God,

Creator of all things

remember that the souls of unbelievers

have been created by Thee

and formed to Thy own image and likeness.

Behold, O Lord,

how to Thy dishonor

hell is being filled with these very souls.

Remember that Jesus Christ, Thy Son

for their salvation suffered a most cruel death.

Do not permit, O Lord,

I beseech Thee

that Thy divine Son

be any longer despised by unbelievers,

but rather,

being appeased by the prayers of Thy saints

and the Church

the most holy spouse of Thy Son

deign to be mindful of Thy mercy

and forgetting their idolatry

and their unbelief

bring them to know Him Whom Thou didst send

Jesus Christ, Thy Son, Our Lord

Who is our health, life, and resurrection

through Whom we have been redeemed and saved

to Whom be all glory forever.

Amen.

Priest:

Pray for us, Saint Francis Xavier,

People:

That we may be made worthy of the promises of Christ.

Priest:

O God, Who did deign,

by the preaching and miracles

of Saint Francis Xavier,

to join unto Thy Church

the nations of the Indies,

grant, we beseech Thee,

that we who reverence his glorious merits,

may also imitate his example,

through Jesus Christ, Our Lord.

Amen.

NOVENA OF SURRENDER TO THE WILL OF GOD

DAY 1

Why do you confuse yourselves by worrying?

Leave the care of your affairs to me

and everything will be peaceful.

I say to you in truth that every act of true,

blind, complete surrender to me

produces the effect that you desire

and resolves all difficult situations.

Repeat 10 times...

O Jesus, I surrender myself to you,

take care of everything!

DAY 2

Surrender to me does not mean to fret,

to be upset, or to lose hope,

nor does it mean offering to me a worried prayer

asking me to follow you

and change your worry into prayer.

It is against this surrender,

deeply against it, to worry,

to be nervous

and to desire to think about the consequences of anything.

It is like the confusion that children feel

when they ask their mother to see to their needs,

and then try to take care of those needs for themselves

so that their childlike efforts get in their mother's way.

Surrender means to placidly close the eyes of the soul,

to turn away from thoughts of tribulation

and to put yourself in my care,

Repeat 10 times...

O Jesus, I surrender myself to you,

take care of everything!

DAY 3

How many things I do when the soul,

in so much spiritual and material need turns to me,

looks at me and says to me;

"You take care of it,"

then close its eyes and rests.

In pain you pray for me to act,

but that I act in the way you want.

You do not turn to me, instead,

you want me to adapt to your ideas.

You are not sick people who ask the doctor to cure you,

but rather sick people who tell the doctor how to.

So do not act this way,

but pray as I taught you in the Our Father:

"Hallowed be thy Name",

that is, be glorified in my need.

"Thy kingdom come",

that is, let all that is in us

and in the world be in accord with your kingdom.

"Thy will be done on Earth as it is in Heaven",

that is, in our need,

decide as you see fit for our temporal and eternal life.

If you say to me truly:

"Thy will be done"

which is the same as saying:

"You take care of it"

I will intervene with all my omnipotence,

and I will resolve the most difficult situations.

Repeat 10 times...

O Jesus, I surrender myself to you,

take care of everything!

DAY 4

You see evil growing instead of weakening?

Do not worry,

Close your eyes and say to me with faith:

"Thy will be done, You take care of it."

I say to you that I will take care of it,

and that I will intervene as does a doctor

and I will accomplish miracles when they are needed.

Do you see that the sick person is getting worse?

Do not be upset,

but close your eyes and say

"You take care of it."

I say to you that I will take care of it,

and that there is no medicine

more powerful than my loving intervention.

By my love, I promise this to you.

Repeat 10 times...

O Jesus, I surrender myself to you,

take care of everything!

DAY 5

And when I must lead you on a path different from the one you see,

I will prepare you;

I will carry you in my arms;

I will let you find yourself,

like children who have fallen asleep in their mother's arms,

on the other bank of the river.

What troubles you and hurts you immensely are your reason,

your thoughts and worry,

and your desire at all costs to deal with what afflicts you.

Repeat 10 times...

O Jesus, I surrender myself to you,

take care of everything!

DAY 6

You are sleepless;

you want to judge everything,

direct everything and see to everything

and you surrender to human strength,

or worse - to men themselves,

trusting in their intervention,

- this is what hinders my words and my views.

Oh how much I wish from you this surrender,

to help you and how I suffer when I see you so agitated!

Satan tries to do exactly this:

to agitate you and to remove you from my protection

and to throw you into the jaws of human initiative.

So, trust only in me,

rest in me,

surrender to me in everything.

Repeat 10 times...

O Jesus, I surrender myself to you,

take care of everything!

DAY 7

I perform miracles in proportion to your full surrender to me

and to your not thinking of yourselves.

I sow treasure troves of graces when you are in the deepest poverty.

No person of reason, no thinker,

has ever performed miracles,

not even among the saints.

He does divine works whosoever surrenders to God.

So don't think about it any more,

because your mind is acute

and for you it is very hard to see evil

and to trust in me

and to not think of yourself.

Do this for all your needs,

do this all of you

and you will see great continual silent miracles.

I will take care of things,

I promise this to you.

Repeat 10 times...

O Jesus, I surrender myself to you,

take care of everything!

DAY 8

Close your eyes and let yourself be carried away

on the flowing current of my grace;

close your eyes and do not think of the present,

turning your thoughts away from the future

just as you would from temptation.

Repose in me, believing in my goodness,

and I promise you by my love that if you say

"You take care of it," I will take care of it all;

I will console you,

liberate you and guide you.

Repeat 10 times...

O Jesus, I surrender myself to you,

take care of everything!

DAY 9

Pray always in readiness to surrender,

and you will receive from it great peace and great rewards,

even when I confer on you the grace of immolation,

of repentance and of love.

Then what does suffering matter?

It seems impossible to you?

Close your eyes and say with all your soul,

"Jesus, you take care of it."

Do not be afraid, I will take care of things

and you will bless my name by humbling yourself.

A thousand prayers cannot equal one single act of surrender,

remember this well.

There is no novena more effective than this:

Repeat 10 times...

O Jesus, I surrender myself to you,

take care of everything!

Mother, I am yours now and forever.

Through you and with you

I always want to belong completely to Jesus.

NOVENA OF THE 24 GLORY BE TO THE FATHER

"Holy Trinity, God the Father, God the Son, and God the Holy Ghost,

I thank Thee for all the blessings and favors

Thou hast showered upon the soul of Thy servant Theresa of the Child Jesus,

during the twenty-four years she spent here on earth,

and in consideration of the merits of this Thy most beloved Saint,

I beseech Thee to grant me this favor,

if it is in accordance with Thy most Holy Will

and is not an obstacle to my salvation."

After this Prayer follows the twenty-four "Glory Be...,"

between each of which may be included this short prayer:

"Saint Theresa of the Child Jesus, pray for us."

THE GLORY BE

Glory be to the Father,

and to the Son,

and to the Holy Ghost.

As it was in the beginning,

is now, and ever shall be,

world without end.

Amen.

Note:

The Twenty-four "Glory be to the Father" Novena can be said at any time. However, the ninth to the seventeenth of the month is particularly recommended, for on those days the petitioner joins in prayer with all those making the Novena.

The "Glory be to the Father" praising the Holy Trinity is said twenty-four times each of the nine days, in thanksgiving for all the blessings and favors given to Saint Theresa of the Child Jesus during the twenty-four years of her life. In addition, the above prayer, or a similar prayer may be said.

NOVENA OF THE ASCENSION #1

O Lord Jesus Christ,

who ascended into heaven in glory,

I adore You and praise You

and beg You to ask Your Heavenly Father

to look down in mercy upon us

who still struggle here on earth.

Amen.

Sacred Heart of Jesus,

may Your Kingdom come!

NOVENA OF THE ASCENSION #2

Jesus, I honor You on the feast of Your Ascension into heaven.

I rejoice with all my heart at the glory

into which You entered to reign as King of heaven and earth.

When the struggle of this life is over,

give me the grace to share Your joy

and triumph in heaven for all eternity.

I believe that You entered into Your glorious Kingdom

to prepare a place for me,

for You promised to come again to take me to Yourself.

Grant that I may seek only the joys of Your friendship and love,

so that I may deserve to be united with You in heaven.

In the hour of my own homecoming,

when I appear before Your Father to give an account of my life on earth,

have mercy on me.

Jesus, in Your love for me

You have brought me from evil to good and from misery to happiness.

Give me the grace to rise above my human weakness.

May Your Humanity give me courage in my weakness

and free me from my sins.

Through Your grace,

give me the courage of perseverance

for You have called and justified me by faith.

May I hold fast to the life You have given me

and come to the eternal gifts You promised.

You love me, dear Jesus.

Help me to love You in return.

I ask You to grant this special favor:

(State your intention here...)

By Your unceasing care,

guide my steps toward the life of glory

You have prepared for those who love You.

Make me grow in holiness

and thank You by a life of faithful service.

NOVENA OF THE ASSUMPTION OF THE VIRGIN MARY # 1

Mary, Queen Assumed into Heaven,

I rejoice that after years of heroic martyrdom on earth,

you have at last been taken to the throne

prepared for you in heaven by the Holy Trinity.

Lift my heart with you in the glory of your Assumption

above the dreadful touch of sin and impurity.

Teach me how small earth becomes when viewed from heaven.

Make me realize that death is the triumphant gate

through which I shall pass to your Son,

and that someday my body shall rejoin my soul

in the unending bliss of heaven.

From this earth,

over which I tread as a pilgrim,

I look to you for help.

I ask for this favor:

(State your intention here...)

When my hour of death has come,

lead me safely to the presence of Jesus

to enjoy the vision of my God for all eternity together with you.

NOVENA OF THE ASSUMPTION OF THE VIRGIN MARY # 2

Majestic Queen of Heaven and Mistress of the Angels,

you received from God the power and command

to crush the head of Satan.

Therefore, we humbly beg of you,

send forth the legions of Heaven,

that under your command they may seek out all evil spirits,

engage them everywhere in battle,

curb their pride,

and hurl them back into the pit of hell.

"Who is like unto God?"

With firm confidence we present ourselves before you,

our most loving Mother,

afflicted and troubled as we are,

and we beg you to let us understand the love

you have for us by granting this petition,

if it is according to the Will of God

and profitable for our salvation:

(State your intention here...)

Good and tender Mother,

you shall ever be our hope and the object of our love.

Mother of God,

send forth the Holy Angels to defend us

and drive far from us the cruel foe.

Holy Angels and Archangels,

defend and keep us.

NOVENA OF THE HOLY NAME

Say once a day for 9 days.

O Merciful Jesus,

Who didst in Thy early infancy

commence Thy office of Savior

by shedding Thy Precious Blood,

and assuming for us that Name

which is above all names;

we thank Thee for such early proofs of Thine infinite love.

We venerate Thy sacred Name,

in union with the profound respect of the Angel

who first announced it to the earth,

and unite our affections to the sentiments of tender devotion

which the adorable name of Jesus

has in all ages enkindled in the hearts of Thy Saints.

Animated with a firm faith in Thy unerring word,

and penetrated with confidence in Thy mercy,

we now most humbly remind Thee of the promise Thou hast made,

that where two or three should assemble in Thy Name,

Thou Thyself wouldst be in the midst of them.

Come, then, into the midst of us, most amiable Jesus,

for it is in Thy sacred Name we are here assembled;

come into our hearts,

that we may be governed by Thy holy spirit;

mercifully grant us, through that adorable Name,

which is the joy of Heaven,

the terror of Hell,

the consolation of the afflicted,

and the solid ground of our unlimited confidence,

all the petitions we make in this novena.

Oh! blessed Mother of our Redeemer!

Who didst participate so sensibly in the sufferings of thy dear Son

when He shed His Sacred Blood and assumed for us the Name of Jesus,

obtain for us, through that adorable Name,

the favors we petition in this novena.

Beg also, that the most ardent love

may imprint on our hearts that Sacred Name,

that it may be always in our minds

and frequently on our lips;

that it may be our defense and our refuge

in the temptations and trials of life,

and our consolation and support in the hour of death.

Amen.

NOVENA OF THE MIRACULOUS MEDAL #1

O Immaculate Virgin Mary,

Mother of Our Lord Jesus and our Mother,

penetrated with the most lively confidence

in you all-powerful and never-failing intercession,

manifested so often through the Miraculous Medal,

we your loving and trustful children

implore you to obtain for us the graces

and favors we ask during this novena,

if they be beneficial to our immortal souls,

and the souls for whom we pray.

(State your intention here...)

You know, O Mary,

how often our souls have been

the sanctuaries of you Son who hates iniquity.

Obtain for us then a deep hatred of sin

and that purity of heart which will attach us to God alone

so that our every thought, word and deed

may tend to His greater glory.

Obtain for us also a spirit of prayer and self-denial

that we may recover by penance

what we have lost by sin

and at length attain to that blessed abode

where you are the Queen of angels and of men.

Amen.

NOVENA OF THE MIRACULOUS MEDAL #2

In the name of the Father

and of the Son

and of the Holy Spirit.

Amen.

Come, O Holy Spirit,

fill the hearts of Your faithful,

and kindle in them the fire of Your love.

Send forth Your Spirit,

and they shall be created.

And You shall renew the face of the earth.

O God, who did instruct the hearts
of the faithful by the light of the Holy Spirit,
grant us in the same Spirit
to be truly wise
and ever to rejoice in His consolation,
through Jesus Christ Our Lord.

Amen.

O Mary, conceived without sin,
pray for us who have recourse to you.

O Mary, conceived without sin,
pray for us who have recourse to you.

O Mary, conceived without sin,
pray for us who have recourse to you.

O Lord Jesus Christ,
who has vouchsafed to glorify
by numberless miracles the Blessed Virgin Mary,
immaculate from the first moment of her conception,

grant that all who

devoutly implore her protection on earth,

may eternally enjoy Your presence in heaven,

who, with the Father and Holy Spirit,

live and reign, God,

for ever and ever.

Amen.

O Lord Jesus Christ,

who for the accomplishment of Your greatest works,

have chosen the weak things of the world,

that no flesh may glory in Your sight;

and who for a better

and more widely diffused belief

in the Immaculate Conception of Your Mother,

have wished that the Miraculous Medal

be manifested to Saint Catherine Labouré,

grant, we beseech You,

that filled with like humility,

we may glorify this mystery by word and work.

Amen.

MEMORARE

Remember, O most compassionate Virgin Mary,

that never was it known

that anyone who fled to your protection,

implored your assistance,

or sought your intercession was left unaided.

Inspired with this confidence,

we fly unto you,

O Virgin of Virgins, our Mother;

to you we come;

before you we kneel sinful and sorrowful.

O Mother of the Word Incarnate,

despise not our petitions,

but in your clemency hear and answer them.

Amen.

NOVENA PRAYER

O Immaculate Virgin Mary,

Mother of Our Lord Jesus and our Mother,

penetrated with the most lively confidence

in you all-powerful and never-failing intercession,

manifested so often through the Miraculous Medal,

we your loving and trustful children

implore you to obtain for us the graces

and favors we ask during this novena,

if they be beneficial to our immortal souls,

and the souls for whom we pray.

(State your intention here...)

You know, O Mary,

how often our souls have been

the sanctuaries of you Son who hates iniquity.

Obtain for us then a deep hatred of sin

and that purity of heart which will attach us to God alone

so that our every thought, word and deed

may tend to His greater glory.

Obtain for us also a spirit of prayer and self-denial

that we may recover by penance

what we have lost by sin

and at length attain to that blessed abode

where you are the Queen of angels and of men.

Amen.

AN ACT OF CONSECRATION TO OUR LADY OF THE MIRACULOUS MEDAL

O Virgin Mother of God,

Mary Immaculate,

we dedicate and consecrate ourselves to you

under the title of Our Lady of the Miraculous Medal.

May this Medal be for each one of us

a sure sign of your affection for us

and a constant reminder of our duties toward you.

Ever while wearing it,

may be blessed by your loving protection

and preserved in the grace of your Son.

O most powerful Virgin,

Mother of our Saviour,

keep us close to you every moment of our lives.

Obtain for us, your children,

the grace of a happy death;

so that, in union with you,

we may enjoy the bliss of heaven forever.

Amen.

O Mary, conceived without sin,

pray for us who have recourse to you.

218

O Mary, conceived without sin,

pray for us who have recourse to you.

O Mary, conceived without sin,

pray for us who have recourse to you.

NOVENA PRAYER FOR ANY NECESSITY

DAY 1

O God, come to my assistance.

O Lord, make haste to help me.

Heavenly Father,

you know all things,

and nothing is hidden from you;

in your kindness come to my aid in my present distress,

and grant my humble petition.

In Christ's name I beg your help.

Amen.

Action: Do a kind deed today for someone you meet.

DAY 2

Hear, O Lord, and have pity on me.

O Lord, be my helper.

Father in heaven,

your love for us never falters in spite of our sins and failures.

Please show your mercy and care for me in my difficulty.

For the sake of Christ, our Savior,

have pity of me.

Amen.

Action: Recognize the image of Christ today in those around you.

DAY 3

Lord, be not far from me.

Awake and be vigilant in my defense, my God.

Loving Father,

you are not far from any of us since in you we live,

move and have our being.

Kindly increase my awareness of your presence,

and take care of my pressing need.

Christ, our Lord, assures us you will.

Amen.

Action: For this day, cast all your cares upon the Lord.

DAY 4

Your ways, O Lord, make known to me.

Teach me your paths.

Father almighty,

your ways and mysterious purpose are often hidden from us;

guide me now, I beg you,

in my sorrow, and by your power aid me to know your will.

May I do it in imitation of Christ, our redeemer.

Amen.

Action: Consider seriously today how best you can do God's will.

DAY 5

Now will I arise, says the Lord.

I will grant safety to him who longs for it.

In you, heavenly Father,

I confidently place all my trust.

In your hands I leave all my anxieties with faith in your care for me.

From you alone I away relief because of Christ,

your Son, who pleads for us.

Amen.

Action: For God's sake, help some person today whom you may not like.

DAY 6

O Lord, reprove me not in your anger,

Nor chastise me in your wrath.

Merciful Father,

you know my sins and disobedience,

my weakness and ingratitude which have deserved punishment.

Yet, you are ever ready to forgive,

and gracious to all in trouble.

In Christ's name,

come quickly to help me.

Amen.

Action: Hold back today the harsh word; banish the unkind thought.

DAY 7

The Lord is a stronghold for the oppressed,

A stronghold in time of distress.

Father in heaven,

you never reject those who seek your help,

and are ever ready to comfort the sorrowful.

Have pity on me in my needs,

and rescue me from all my afflictions.

In Christ's name,

I implore your compassion.

Amen.

Action: In imitation of Christ, do good to those who dislike you.

DAY 8

The Lord is close to the brokenhearted,

And those who are crushed in spirit, He saves.

Your goodness, heavenly Father,

responds speedily to our wretchedness.

In my distress I call upon you

to hear and answer my prayers.

In you alone, O God,

I will continue to trust despite everything.

In Christ's name.

Amen.

Action: Help someone you know who needs your aid today.

DAY 9

The Lord came to my support.

He set me free and rescued me because He loves me.

Gracious Father,

I will thank you each day for your merciful goodness to me.

With your help I will ever praise your kindness in my trouble.

Please assist me now in faithfully following Christ, my Savior.

Amen.

Action: In gratitude, be good to others today and always.

NOVENA PRAYER FOR CONVERSION FROM CONTRACEPTION

[A novena of conversion for those who use or promote contraception.]

Heavenly Father,

"from whom every family in heaven and on earth takes its name," (Eph 3:15)

grant conversion of heart to our world,

our society, our families

and especially to our own hearts regarding the sin of contraception.

We believe, beyond a doubt,

what the one, holy, Catholic and apostolic Church

teaches about this moral evil,

and we wish to be a light to the nations

to make the truth known wherever this evil practice and ideology has taken root.

Call us to be faithful to your command to "Be fruitful and multiply!"

so that we may advance the civilization of life and love

that you wish to create for the human family.

Bring to conversion those who, in public or private,

lead others into the sin of contraception

and who erroneously teach that it prevents abortion.

Help us all to be purified of the lies and distortions

of the culture of death by obedience to the truth

and bring us all to the fullness of truth

through the guidance of your Church.

We ask this through the intercession of the Immaculate Virgin Mary,

in whose fertile womb your Blessed Son found his home on earth.

Amen.

GOOD FRIDAY NOVENA PRAYER

Jesus Christ,

Son of God made Man,

crowned with thorns,

bearing a scepter of a reed,

wearing a royal cloak purpled

with Your Precious Blood,

I venerate You as the Man of Sorrows

and acknowledge You as my Lord and King!

Jesus crucified,

I firmly renounce the devil

and detest all sin

that has torn me from Your loving friendship.

I pledge my loyalty to You,

my Saviour,

and beg You to make me Your own in sincerest love.

I promise to be faithful in service to You,

and to strive to become more pleasing to you

by avoiding every sin and its occasions,

by carrying out my duties

perfectly as a good Catholic,

and by practicing virtue.

Jesus crucified,

accept the homage I wish to render You

during this novena,

as a token of my sincerest appreciation

for the sorrows and sufferings

You have willingly borne to atone for my many sins

and to prove how much You love me.

I adore You as my very God,

Who willed to become Man

in order to save me from eternal death.

I thank You as my best Friend,

Who laid down Your life

as proof of the greatest love possible.

I ask pardon for having so little thought of You,

Jesus crucified,

and for having caused Your sorrows

and sufferings by the many sins I have committed.

I pray to You,

dearest Jesus,

for all the graces I need to know You,

to love You and serve You faithfully unto death,

and to save my soul.

Give me a tender and fervent devotion

to Your Sacred Passion by which I was redeemed,

venerating You especially in Holy Mass.

Teach me how to unite sorrows and sufferings

of my life with Your own.

Finally, through all Your sorrows and pains,

through Your Sacred Heart

glowing with love for me,

broken because of my want of love for You,

through the sorrows of Mary,

your Sorrowful Mother,

I ask for this special favor:

[Mention your request here...]

With childlike trust

I abandon myself to Your holy Will

concerning my request.

NOVENA PRAYER FOR LIFE TO OUR LADY OF GUADALUPE.

Oh Mary, Mother of Jesus and Mother of Life,

We honor you as Our Lady of Guadalupe.

Thank you for pointing us to Jesus your Son,

The only Savior and hope of the world.

Renew our hope in him,

That we all may have the courage to say Yes to life,

And to defend those children in danger of abortion.

Give us your compassion

To reach out to those tempted to abort,

And to those suffering from a past abortion.

Lead us to the day when abortion

Will be a sad, past chapter in our history.

Keep us close to Jesus, the Life of the World,

Who is Lord forever and ever.

Amen.

NOVENA PRAYER TO THE IMMACULATE HEART OF MARY

O Most Blessed Mother,

heart of love,

heart of mercy,

ever listening,

caring, consoling,

hear our prayer.

As your children,

we implore your intercession

with Jesus your Son.

Receive with understanding and compassion

the petitions we place before you today,

especially...

(State your request here...)

We are comforted in knowing your heart

is ever open to those who ask for your prayer.

We trust to your gentle care and intercession,

those whom we love

and who are sick

or lonely

or hurting.

Help all of us,

Holy Mother,

to bear our burdens in this life

until we may share eternal life

and peace with God forever.

Amen.

NOVENA PRAYER TO THE SACRED HEART

May the Sacred Heart of Jesus be adored and loved

in all the tabernacles until the end of time.

Amen.

May the Most Sacred Heart of Jesus

be praised and glorified now and forever.

Amen.

Blessed be the Sacred Heart of Jesus.

Blessed be the Immaculate Heart of Mary.

Sacred Heart of Jesus,

Pray for us and hear our prayer.

Amen.

NOVENA ROSE PRAYER

O Little Thérèse of the Child Jesus,

please pick for me a rose

from the heavenly gardens

and send it to me as a message of love.

O Little Flower of Jesus,

ask God today to grant the favors

I now place with confidence in your hands...

(Make your request here...)

St. Thérèse,

help me to always believe as you did,

in God's great love for me,

so that I might imitate

your "Little Way" each day.

Amen

NOVENA TO SAINT KATERI TEKAKWITHA

Kateri, favored child and Lily of the Mohawks,

I come to seek your intercession in my present need:

(State your intention here...)

I admire the virtues which adorned your soul:

love of God and neighbor,

humility, obedience, patience,

purity and the spirit of sacrifice.

Help me to imitate your example in my state of life.

Through the goodness and mercy of God,

Who has blessed you with so many graces

which led you to the true faith

and to a high degree of holiness,

pray to God for me and help me.

Obtain for me a very fervent devotion to the Holy Eucharist

so that I may love Holy Mass as you did

and receive Holy Communion as often as I can.

Teach me also to be devoted

to my crucified Savior as you were,

that I may cheerfully bear my daily crosses

for love of Him Who suffered so much for love of me.

Most of all I beg you to pray for me

that I may avoid sin,

lead a holy life and save my soul.

AMEN

In Thanksgiving to God for the graces bestowed upon Kateri:

(Recite the following prayers...)

Our Father...

Hail Mary...

Glory Be... (3 times)

Kateri, Lily of the Mohawks,

pray for me.

NOVENA TO BLESSED MARGARET OF CASTELLO

FIRST DAY

O Blessed Margaret of Castello,

In embracing your life just as it was,

You gave us an example of resignation

To the Will of god.

In so accepting God's Will,

You knew that you would grow in virtue,

Glorify God, save your own soul,

And help the souls of your neighbors.

Obtain for me the grace,

To recognize the will of God,

In all that may happen to me in my life,

And so resign myself to it.

Obtain for me also the special favor,

Which I now ask,

Through your intercession with God.

Let us pray…

O God by whose Will

The blessed virgin, Margaret,

Was blind from birth,

That the eyes of her mind

Being inwardly enlightened

She might think without ceasing

On You alone;

Be the light of our eyes,

That we may be able

To flee the shadows in this world,

And reach the home

Of never-ending light.

We ask this through Christ our Lord.

Amen.

Jesus, Mary, Joseph,

Glorify your servant blessed Margaret,

By granting the favor

We so ardently desire.

This we ask in humble submission

To God's Will,

For His Honor and Glory

And the salvation of souls.

Our Father...

Hail Mary...

Glory Be...

SECOND DAY

O Blessed Margaret of Castello,

In reflecting so deeply

Upon the sufferings and death

Of our Crucified Lord,

You learned courage

And gained the grace

To bear your own afflictions.

Obtain for me

The grace and courage

That I so urgently need

So as to be able to bear

My infirmities and endure my afflictions

In union with our Suffering Savior.

Obtain for me also

The special favor which I now ask

Through your intercession with God.

Let us pray…

O God by whose Will

The blessed virgin, Margaret,

Was blind from birth,

That the eyes of her mind

Being inwardly enlightened

She might think without ceasing

On You alone;

Be the light of our eyes,

That we may be able

To flee the shadows in this world,

And reach the home

Of never-ending light.

We ask this through Christ our Lord.

Amen.

Jesus, Mary, Joseph,

Glorify your servant blessed Margaret,

By granting the favor

We so ardently desire.

This we ask in humble submission

To God's Will,

For His Honor and Glory

And the salvation of souls.

Our Father...

Hail Mary...

Glory Be...

THIRD DAY

O Blessed Margaret of Castello,

Your love for Jesus

In the Blessed Sacrament

Was intense and enduring.

It was here

In intimacy with the Divine Presence

That you found spiritual strength

To accept suffering,

To be cheerful, patient and kindly

Towards others.

Obtain for me the grace

That I may draw from this same source,

As from an exhaustible font,

The strength whereby I may be

Kind and understanding

Of everyone despite whatever pain or discomfort

May come my way.

Obtain for your intercession with God.

Let us pray…

O God by whose Will

The blessed virgin, Margaret,

Was blind from birth,

That the eyes of her mind

Being inwardly enlightened

She might think without ceasing

On You alone;

Be the light of our eyes,

That we may be able

To flee the shadows in this world,

And reach the home

Of never-ending light.

We ask this through Christ our Lord.

Amen.

Jesus, Mary, Joseph,

Glorify your servant blessed Margaret,

By granting the favor

We so ardently desire.

This we ask in humble submission

To God's Will,

For His Honor and Glory

And the salvation of souls.

Our Father...

Hail Mary...

Glory Be...

FOURTH DAY

O Blessed Margaret of Castello,

You unceasingly turned to God in prayer

With confidence and trust

In His Fatherly love.

It was only through continual prayer

That you were enabled

To accept your misfortunes,

To be serene, patient, and at peace.

Obtain for me the grace

To persevere in my prayer,

Confident that God will give me

The help to carry whatever cross

Comes into my life.

Obtain for me also the special favor

Which I now ask

Through your intercession with God.

Let us pray…

O God by whose Will

The blessed virgin, Margaret,

Was blind from birth,

That the eyes of her mind

Being inwardly enlightened

She might think without ceasing

On You alone;

Be the light of our eyes,

That we may be able

To flee the shadows in this world,

And reach the home

Of never-ending light.

We ask this through Christ our Lord.

Amen.

Jesus, Mary, Joseph,

Glorify your servant blessed Margaret,

By granting the favor

We so ardently desire.

This we ask in humble submission

To God's Will,

For His Honor and Glory

And the salvation of souls.

Our Father...

Hail Mary...

Glory Be...

FIFTH DAY

O Blessed Margaret of Castello,

In imitation of the Child Jesus,

Who was subject to Mary and Joseph,

You obeyed your father and mother,

Overlooking their unnatural harshness.

Obtain for me

That same attitude of obedience

Toward all those

Who have legitimate authority over me,

Most especially toward

The Holy Roman Catholic Church.

Obtain for me also

The special favor which I now ask

Through your intercession with God.

Let us pray…

O God by whose Will

The blessed virgin, Margaret,

Was blind from birth,

That the eyes of her mind

Being inwardly enlightened

She might think without ceasing

On You alone;

Be the light of our eyes,

That we may be able

To flee the shadows in this world,

And reach the home

Of never-ending light.

We ask this through Christ our Lord.

Amen.

Jesus, Mary, Joseph,

Glorify your servant blessed Margaret,

By granting the favor

We so ardently desire.

This we ask in humble submission

To God's Will,

For His Honor and Glory

And the salvation of souls.

Our Father...

Hail Mary...

Glory Be...

SIXTH DAY

O Blessed Margaret of Castello,

Your miseries taught you

Better than any teacher

The weakness and frailty

Of human nature.

Obtain for me

The grace to recognize

My human limitations

And to acknowledge

My utter dependence upon God.

Acquire for me

That abandonment which leaves me

Completely at the mercy of God

To do with me whatsoever He wills.

Obtain for me also

The special favor which I now ask

Through your intercession with God.

Let us pray…

O God by whose Will

The blessed virgin, Margaret,

Was blind from birth,

That the eyes of her mind

Being inwardly enlightened

She might think without ceasing

On You alone;

Be the light of our eyes,

That we may be able

To flee the shadows in this world,

And reach the home

Of never-ending light.

We ask this through Christ our Lord.

Amen.

Jesus, Mary, Joseph,

Glorify your servant blessed Margaret,

By granting the favor

We so ardently desire.

This we ask in humble submission

To God's Will,

For His Honor and Glory

And the salvation of souls.

Our Father...

Hail Mary...

Glory Be...

SEVENTH DAY

O blessed Margaret of Castello,

You could have so easily

Become discouraged and bitter;

But, instead, you fixed your eyes

On the suffering Christ

And there you learned from Him

The redemptive value of suffering -

How to offer your pains and aches,

In reparation for sin

And for the salvation of souls.

Obtain for me the grace

To learn how to endure

My sufferings with patience.

Obtain for me also

The special favor which I now ask

Through your intercession with God.

Let us pray…

O God by whose Will

The blessed virgin, Margaret,

Was blind from birth,

That the eyes of her mind

Being inwardly enlightened

She might think without ceasing

On You alone;

Be the light of our eyes,

That we may be able

To flee the shadows in this world,

And reach the home

Of never-ending light.

We ask this through Christ our Lord.

Amen.

Jesus, Mary, Joseph,

Glorify your servant blessed Margaret,

By granting the favor

We so ardently desire.

This we ask in humble submission

To God's Will,

For His Honor and Glory

And the salvation of souls.

Our Father...

Hail Mary...

Glory Be...

EIGHTH DAY

O Blessed Margaret of Castello,

How it must have hurt

When your parents abandoned you!

Yet you learned from this

That all earthly love and affection,

Even for those who are closest,

Must be sanctified.

And so, despite everything,

You continued to love your parents –

But now you loved them in God.

Obtain for me the grace

That I might see

All my human loves and affections

In their proper perspective…

In God and for god. Obtain for me also

The special favor which I now ask

Through your intercession with God.

Let us pray…

O God by whose Will

The blessed virgin, Margaret,

Was blind from birth,

That the eyes of her mind

Being inwardly enlightened

She might think without ceasing

On You alone;

Be the light of our eyes,

That we may be able

To flee the shadows in this world,

And reach the home

Of never-ending light.

We ask this through Christ our Lord.

Amen.

Jesus, Mary, Joseph,

Glorify your servant blessed Margaret,

By granting the favor

We so ardently desire.

This we ask in humble submission

To God's Will,

For His Honor and Glory

And the salvation of souls.

Our Father...

Hail Mary...

Glory Be...

NINTH DAY

O Blessed Margaret of Castello,

Through your suffering and misfortune,

You became sensitive

To the sufferings of others.

Your heart reached out

To everyone in trouble –

The sick, the hungry, the dying prisoners.

Obtain for me the grace

To recognize Jesus in everyone

With whom I come into contact,

Especially in the poor,

The wretched, the unwanted!

Obtain for me also

The special favor which I now ask

Through your intercession with God.

Let us pray…

O God by whose Will

The blessed virgin, Margaret,

Was blind from birth,

That the eyes of her mind

Being inwardly enlightened

She might think without ceasing

On You alone;

Be the light of our eyes,

That we may be able

To flee the shadows in this world,

And reach the home

Of never-ending light.

We ask this through Christ our Lord.

Amen.

Jesus, Mary, Joseph,

Glorify your servant blessed Margaret,

By granting the favor

We so ardently desire.

This we ask in humble submission

To God's Will,

For His Honor and Glory

And the salvation of souls.

Our Father...

Hail Mary...

Glory Be...

Prayer

O my God, I thank you

For having given

Blessed Margaret of Castello

To the world as an example

Of the degree of holiness

That can be attained by anyone

Who truly loves you,

Regardless of physical abnormalities.

In today's perverted culture,

Margaret would have, most likely,

Never been born;

Death through abortion

Being preferable to life,

Especially life

In an ugly distorted twisted body.

But Your ways are not the world's ways…

And so it was Your Will

That Margaret would be born into the world

With just such a malformed body.

It is Your way that uses our weakness

To give testimony to Your power.

Margaret was born blind,

So as to see You more clearly;

A cripple, so as to lean on You completely;

Dwarfed in physical posture,

So as to become a giant in the spiritual order;

Hunch-backed,

So as to more perfectly resemble

The twisted, crucified body of Your Son.

Margaret's whole life

Was an enactment of the words

Expressed by Paul:

"So I shall be very happy

To make my weaknesses my special boast

So that the power of Christ may stay over me

And that is why I am content

With my weaknesses,

And with insults, hardships,

Persecutions and the agonies

I go through for Christ's sake.

For it is when I am weak that I am strong." (2 Cor 12:10).

I beseech you, O God,

To grant through the intercession

Of Blessed Margaret of Castello,

That all the handicapped …

And who among us is not?…

All rejected, all unwanted of the world

May make their weaknesses

Their own special boast

So that your power may stay over them

Now and forever.

Amen.

Blessed Margaret of Castello, pray for us.

Our Father...

Hail Mary...

Our Father...

Hail Mary...

Our Father...

Hail Mary...

NOVENA TO CHRIST THE KING

Say the following prayers each day:

O Lord our God,

You alone are the Most Holy King and Ruler of all nations.

We pray to You, Lord,

in the great expectation of receiving from You,

O Divine King, mercy, peace, justice and all good things.

Protect, O Lord our King, our families and the land of our birth.

Guard us we pray Most Faithful One.

Protect us from our enemies and from Your Just Judgment

Forgive us, O Sovereign King, our sins against you.

Jesus, You are a King of Mercy.

We have deserved Your Just Judgment

Have mercy on us, Lord, and forgive us.

We trust in Your Great Mercy.

O most awe-inspiring King, we bow before You and pray;

May Your Reign, Your Kingdom, be recognized on earth.

Amen.

Our Father...

Hail Mary...

Glory Be...

NOVENA TO GOD THE FATHER #1

FOREWORD

The humanity of the third millennium is facing problems which can be resolved only by global cooperation. Many people look forward to the future with anxiety and sorrow. To become aware that we are one great family of men is more urgent than ever before.

Isn't it time to discover the real base of human brotherhood, that is to say, the universal paternity of God? It is an immense task in which Christians have a primordial role to play. It is we who have to begin to better live our real identity, Christian and human: that is to be children of the same Father through Christ in the Spirit.

Devotion to the Father was the devotion of Jesus. The whole person of Jesus is polarized by the Father. His mission is to reveal to us the Father, to manifest His infinite love, to open the way and lead us to Him. Yet the manner in which Jesus spoke to his Father was revolutionary: "Abba," or "Dad," as a little child calls his father.

The first Christians exclaimed "Abba, dear Father!" in the enthusiasm of the Holy Spirit, expressing their new life as children of God. Presently are we really with Jesus on the way to the Father? Or have we become "fatherless" after the criticism of the father figure by psychoanalysts and feminists? Not at all, provided that we are conscious first that God the Father is not a man but God; and second that we mean what Jesus meant by "Father", namely

God as the Origin of Total, Infinite and Unconditional Goodness. Then we can call God "Father", or even like Jesus, "Abba" or " Dad" in childlike simplicity.

May these prayers help us to enter the stream of filial love of Christ and so serve the grandiose design of the Father: reunite all human beings into one family in Christ "for the praise of his glory". (Eph 1,12)

FIRST DAY

You are Only Love

See what love the Father has given us… [1 Jn. 3:1]

Father, how wonderful! With you all is so simple.

Before you, I can be like a child.

I can ask you for everything, and you give me all I need.

I can tell you without fear, whatever l like.

You listen to me. I am important to you.

You understand me.

You never grow tired of me. You never turn away from me.

At all times you are entirely present to me.

You don't regard my fortune, my knowledge, my performance.

You accept me as I am.

You don't look at my faults.

You don't condemn me.

You pardon me everything, and you don't bear me any grudge.

You take me as I am now, not as I have been,

and you permit me always to begin again.

From you I have nothing to fear.

You are the Father of all of us.

Whoever wants can come to you, no one is excluded.

You love everyone with the same love, even more than that:

you love everyone as your own Son.

Father, how unheard of, how unbelievable all this sounds!

However it is true.

Jesus has testified that you really are so:

Love, infinite Love.

Our Father...

SECOND DAY

The Greatest Gift

If you then, who are evil,

know how to give good gifts to your children,

how much more will the heavenly Father give the Holy Spirit to those who ask him! [Lk. 11:13]

Father, all good gifts come from you.

The greater and more precious the gift is,

the more gladly you want to give it to us.

Therefore, dear Father,

I want to ask you today for the greatest and best of all gifts:

For love, for the Holy Spirit.

Father, I need the Holy Spirit.

I want to live, to enjoy life without having to fear death.

I would like to keep my spirit young and flexible.

I want to become generous, compassionate and ready to help.

I wish to become free from all that burdens me,

what is inhibiting me or making a slave out of me.

I want to defeat my indifference, my laziness,

my anxiety, my discouragement and my sadness

I need strength for suffering, for pardoning, for rising again.

I would like to become a new creature

and contribute that the world becomes a little more human.

It's You, who have put these desires in our heart.

It is your joy to fulfill them in giving us the Holy Spirit.

Send out your Spirit who makes us your children,

who hallows your name by crying in us "Abba, dear Father!"

Grant me that I don't cease to pray again and again: Come, Holy Spirit!

Our Father...

THIRD DAY

Your Heart's Desire

He destined us in Love to be his sons through Jesus Christ [Eph. 1:5]

Dear Father, from eternity you have thought of us.

Your loving heart concealed a wonderful plan:

You wanted to raise children, loving them in your Son and as your Son.

With a holy enthusiasm you have created the universe with this aim.

You will one great family in which all would be united

in the love of Christ as brothers and sisters.

This community of love is your Church.

All in it is founded on love.

That's why all in it shall be accomplished by love, in love and for love.

What a dream! A community which knows only love and is open to all men.

Father, this dream shall become reality!

I will begin just where I am:

Let me consider my neighbor as this whom Jesus wants to love through me.

Make me patient, comprehensive, large-hearted,

considering others better than myself,

everywhere emphasizing what is good,

abstaining from loveless criticism of others.

May I keep only those thoughts in my mind which serve love and unity,

and endeavor to make peace.

Father, let the Church more and more resemble the Trinitarian Communion of Love!

Our Father...

FOURTH DAY

Only Love Matters

If I have not love, I am nothing. [Cor. 13:2]

Father, your will is love, for you are love,

unconditional, unlimited love – and only love.

Father, all love comes from you.

Fill my heart and hand with love, goodness and mercy,

and let these overflow upon everyone of my fellow-men.

You want that I love you in my fellow-creatures.

I am not closer to you than I am to my neighbor, even to my greatest enemy.

Let me be so cheerful and kind

that all I meet feel your presence and your love.

Help me to love everyone as I wish to be loved.

Give me the power to repay evil with good.

Allow me to love myself too, with all my deficiencies,

weakness and limits, as you love me.

Let me consider everything as an occasion

to love and answer everything with love:

what is obscure and incomprehensible, with faith and confidence;

sickness and need, with help and consolation;

hatred and spite, with goodness and forgiveness;

injustice and oppression, with courageous involvement for justice and freedom.

Only love matters.

I am born to love.

Love is my vocation.

So I ask you only for this: for love, for still more love.

Our Father...

FIFTH DAY

You Take Care of Us

Your Father knows what you need [Mt. 6:8]

Father, I don't know what life will bring me yet.

The future is hidden to us. Will I always have a job? How will my health be?

What will the future of the Church be? Where is the world going?

You don't want us to be troubled, for you take care of us.

You are our Father and we are your children.

A child cannot earn his living. It cannot maintain itself.

It depends on others.

Father, could I exist without you?

What is my own that I haven't received from you?

Finally I owe all to you, my kindly Father.

Only you know the future. You know everything,

you have power over all and you love me.

That's why with you I can feel myself totally safe.

Father, I abandon all to you.

As you ordain it, that is best for me.

I believe in your love.

I believe that you always assist your Church with your Spirit

and that you guide us by our shepherds in good pasture.

You love our earth.

That's why I believe that you will also grant it a future.

Father, I trust you entirely.

I am still wanting only one thing:

to answer your love with gratitude

and to please you with my confidence and simplicity.

All for your greater joy!

Our Father...

SIXTH DAY

Forgive Me

Father, forgive them; for they know not what they do. [Lk. 23:34]

Father, I have failed against love.

I was self-righteous, lacking in generosity, and ungrateful.

For you, our offenses are not an affront to your honor.

What hurts you is, that by our sin, we act against our own well-being.

You are not concerned about your honor

which was violated but only about the happiness of your children.

Father, I am so sorry that I didn't listen to the appeal of your love.

I am aware that I cannot claim your pardon if I myself do not pardon others.

But my negative feelings still remain.

However, you do not look on what we are feeling

but only on what we are willing to do.

Father, I am resolved to forgive everyone who trespassed against me,

and I will pray for them.

Pardon me too all my trespasses.

I regret them from the bottom of my heart.

I can be sure that you pardon me,

for seeing your child return to you is your greatest joy.

Father, preserve me from judging others,

being irreconcilable and resentful.

Let me always remember that Jesus pardoned even those who crucified him.

Father, I thank you for your love, and I praise your infinite mercy.

Our Father...

SEVENTH DAY

In spite of suffering I believe in your love

This slight momentary affliction is preparing for us

an eternal weight of glory beyond all comparison. [2 Cor. 4:17]

Father, when it becomes gloomy in my soul,

don't let me think that you are no longer with me.

If I am afflicted by sickness or harm,

don't let me think that you want to punish me for something.

If I have fallen into sin and guilt,

don't let me believe that you are angry with me

and that you won't love me any longer.

If I feel useless and weak,

don't let me think that I don't count for you any more.

Aren't you then especially near to me since you are love?

Can I do anything greater than to accept suffering and to say:

Father, I love you?

The greatest performance is suffering and the greatest action is love.

What could Jesus still do on the cross?

Nothing else than suffer and love.

It was not you who wanted his suffering, for you are love.

But you have turned all into the best:

into life and salvation for the whole world,

into victory over sin and death,

into glory without end for all those who have opened their hearts to love.

Father, I believe in your almighty power and infinite love.

You have done what is best for your children.

All is an occasion for love.

You are able to turn the greatest evil into greatest good.

Into your hands I put everything that I have and that I am.

Not my will shall be done but yours, always and everywhere.

Father, I love you!

Our Father...

EIGHTH DAY

Home to you

Even though I walk through the valley of the shadow of death, I fear no evil;

for thou art with me... [Ps. 23 (22), 4]

Father, time is passing away. I am growing older and older.

My forces decrease. I am going towards my death.

Shall I be sad about it?

No, every moment that passes draws me nearer to you.

Though my outer nature is wasting away,

my inner nature is being renewed every day by your love.

Your love doesn't fade away but is eternal youth, beauty, power and freshness.

That's why I can continue my way with joy and confidence.

I can be certain of your love and have nothing to fear,

neither have I to fear even you.

Your justice is not in opposition to your goodness.

It is not revenging, repaying justice like ours but one which makes all just.

It doesn't put to death but brings to life.

Your justice is your holiness - and holiness is love.

In your eyes sin is sickness. So you are not like a judge in front of the accused,

but like a mother or father at the bed of a child who is sick.

Father, help me cling to nothing but you, that I take nothing for important except love.

Let me become more and more simple, devote, grateful,

joyful until the summit of my life

where I can give myself entirely to you and enter into your house forever.

Our Father...

NINTH DAY

Heavenly Joy

Give thanks to the Father, who has qualified us

to share in the inheritance of the saints in light. [Col. 1:12]

Heavenly Father, how few there are who look forward to heaven!

Heaven seems not to interest people…or, on the contrary,

are they interested in anything else than in heaven?

The whole world is looking for joy, happiness and bliss.

Father, you have created us for joy because you are love.

Love wants to give joy.

What can a father wish more than to see cheerful children?

In our joys your Heart is uncovering itself.

The enjoyment of the goods of our earth

allows us to experience who you are:

goodness, unlimited goodness.

Heaven has already begun! All the joys you give us are messengers of heaven.

All your commands are signposts to heaven.

Already we can spread around us a little heaven through our love and goodness.

Already we can cordially rejoice with you,

with each other and all your creatures, and sing the praise of your glory.

How beautiful it will be once we are in heaven! You will wipe away every tear.

No guilt, no suffering, no death will be any more.

Forever only one thing will fill our heart and make us perfectly happy: Love.

Praise to you, Father so good, who has made us your children!

Praise to your Son, joy of the world, in whom you reveal to us your true face!

Praise to the Spirit, jubilation of love, in whom we cry:

Abba, dear Father!

NOVENA TO GOD THE FATHER #2

God, my heavenly Father, I adore You,

and I count myself as nothing before Your Divine Majesty.

You alone are Being, Life, Truth, and Goodness.

Helpless and unworthy as i am, I honor You,

I praise You, I thank You,

and I love You in union with Jesus Christ, Your Son,

our Savior and our Brother,

in the merciful kindness of His Heart and through His infinite merits.

I desire to serve You, to please You, to obey You,

and to love You always in union with Mary Immaculate,

Mother of God and our Mother.

I also desire to love and serve my neighbor for the love of You.

Heavenly Father, thank You for making me Your child in Baptism.

With childlike confidence I ask You for this special favor:

[State your intention(s) here...]

I ask that Your Will may be done.

Give me what You know to be best for my soul,

and for the souls of those for whom I pray.

Give me Your Holy Spirit to enlighten me, to correct me,

and to guide me in the way of Your commandments and holiness,

while I strive for the happiness of heaven

where I hope to glorify You forever.

Amen.

NOVENA TO MARIA BAMBINA

Holy Child Mary of the royal house of David, Queen of the angels,

Mother of grace and love, I greet you with all my heart.

Obtain for me the grace to love the Lord faithfully during

all the days of my life. Obtain for me, too, a great devotion to you, who are the first creature of God's love.

Pray the "Hail Mary..."

O heavenly Child Mary, who like a pure dove was born
immaculate and beautiful, true prodigy of the wisdom of
God, my soul rejoices in you. Oh! Do help me to preserve
the angelic virtue of purity at the cost of any sacrifice.

Pray the "Hail Mary..."

Hail, lovely and holy Child, spiritual garden of delight, where,
on the day of the Incarnation, the tree of life was planted,
assist me to avoid the poisonous fruit of vanity and pleasures of the world.
Help me to engraft into my soul the thoughts, feelings,
and virtues of your divine Son.

Pray the "Hail Mary..."

Hail, admirable Child Mary, Mystical Rose, closed garden,
open only to the heavenly Spouse. O Lily of paradise,

make me love the humble and hidden life;

let the heavenly Spouse find the gate of my heart always open

to the loving calls of His graces and inspiration.

Pray the "Hail Mary..."

Holy Child Mary, mystical dawn, gate of heaven,

you are my trust and hope.

O powerful advocate, from your cradle stretch out your hand,

support me on the path of life.

Make me serve God with ardor and

constancy until death and so reach an eternity with you.

Pray the "Hail Mary..."

Prayer

Blessed Child Mary,

destined to be the Mother of God

and our loving Mother,

by the heavenly graces you lavish upon us,

mercifully listen to my supplications.

In the needs which press upon me from every side

and especially in my present tribulation,

I place all my trust in you.

O holy Child,

by the privileges granted to you alone

and by the merits which you have acquired,

show that the source of spiritual favors

and the continuous benefits

which you dispense are inexhaustible,

because your power with the Heart of God is unlimited.

Deign through the immense profusion of graces

with which the Most High has enriched you

from the first moment of your Immaculate Conception,

grant me, O Celestial Child, my petition,

and I shall eternally praise

the goodness of your Immaculate Heart.

NOVENA TO MARY, QUEEN OF APOSTLES

DAY ONE

"I will put enmity between you and the woman,

and between your offspring and hers;

he will strike your head,

and you will strike his heel" (Gen 3:15).

Through God's loving foresight,

Mary was placed, so to speak,

on a path different from that on which

all the common children of Eve,

born with original sin,

entered the world.

The new path is that of the redeemed.

The light of the cross illumined Mary's conception,

infancy and youth.

Thus, she was worthy to be blessed among women.

Together let us honor Mary Immaculate,

Queen of Apostles,

and ask her to give Jesus Master,

Way, Truth and Life,

to all of us and to all people on earth.

Reflection and Resolution

Prayer:

O God, you sent the Holy Spirit upon the apostles

as they were united in prayer with Mary,

the Mother of Jesus.

May the Queen of Apostles,

the same Mother of us all,

help us to serve your majesty faithfully,

and to spread the glory of Your Name

by word and example.

Through Christ our Lord.

Amen.

"Our Father..."

"Hail Mary..."

"Glory be..."

Queen of Apostles,

pray for us.

DAY TWO

"The Holy Spirit will come upon you,

and the power of the Most High will overshadow you;

therefore the child to be born will be holy;

He will be called Son of God" (Lk 1:35).

The grace in a soul is like a root

from which a plant develops with its branches,

leaves, flowers and fruits.

Virtues grow in a soul in proportion to grace.

Thus, we understand why

Mary reached the highest degree of virtue and holiness:

because she was full of grace.

She possessed the theological,

cardinal and moral virtues,

the beatitudes

and the fruits of the Holy Spirit

to an eminent degree.

Mary is full of grace,

the creature most intimate with God,

the Blessed Mother

who gives Jesus to us

and helps us to love him.

She makes us conceive a great fear of sin

and of dangerous occasions.

She inspires in us the desire for purity and for sacrifice.

Reflection and Resolution

Prayer:

O God, you sent the Holy Spirit upon the apostles

as they were united in prayer with Mary,

the Mother of Jesus.

May the Queen of Apostles,

the same Mother of us all,

help us to serve your majesty faithfully,

and to spread the glory of Your Name

by word and example.

Through Christ our Lord.

Amen.

"Our Father..."

"Hail Mary..."

"Glory be..."

Queen of Apostles,

pray for us.

DAY THREE

"She gave birth to her firstborn Son

and wrapped him in bands of cloth,

and laid him in a manger,

because there was no place for them in the inn" (Lk 2:7).

Mary fulfills her apostolate:

to give Jesus to the Father,

to humanity, to heaven.

She presented Jesus to the Gentiles,

represented by the Magi

who came to the crib in Bethlehem.

Mary always gives Jesus.

She is like a fruitful branch.

She always carries Jesus

and offers him to us:

the Way, the Truth and the Life of humanity.

Let us pray to Mary,

the Mother of the infant Jesus,

that through her maternal intercession

we may all welcome the message from the crib:

"Glory to God in the highest heaven,

and on earth peace among those whom he favors!" (Lk 2:14).

Reflection and Resolution

Prayer:

O God, you sent the Holy Spirit upon the apostles

as they were united in prayer with Mary,

the Mother of Jesus.

May the Queen of Apostles,

the same Mother of us all,

help us to serve your majesty faithfully,

and to spread the glory of Your Name

by word and example.

Through Christ our Lord.

Amen.

"Our Father..."

"Hail Mary..."

"Glory be..."

Queen of Apostles,

pray for us.

DAY FOUR

"This child is destined for the falling

and the rising of many in Israel,

and to be a sign that will be opposed...

and a sword will pierce your own soul too" (Lk 2:34-35).

Jesus Christ saw Mary at the foot of his cross,

sharing in His passion.

The Christian possesses an inexhaustible strength

and is able to endure great sufferings without breaking.

In suffering, a person can attain great nobility of character;

indeed, suffering becomes a real apostolate.

Let us always trustfully invoke Mary:

"Pray for us,

now and at the hour of our death."

All to Mary, from Mary, with Mary.

She shows everyone on earth her Son.

Let us pray:

"After this our exile,

show to us the blessed fruit of your womb, Jesus."

Reflection and Resolution

Prayer:

O God, you sent the Holy Spirit upon the apostles

as they were united in prayer with Mary,

the Mother of Jesus.

May the Queen of Apostles,

the same Mother of us all,

help us to serve your majesty faithfully,

and to spread the glory of Your Name

by word and example.

Through Christ our Lord.

Amen.

"Our Father..."

"Hail Mary..."

"Glory be..."

Queen of Apostles,

pray for us.

DAY FIVE

"His mother treasured all these things in her heart" (Lk 2:51).

The presentation of the Lord enlightens us

to live in holiness,

detachment from worldly things,

and purity of thoughts and actions.

The child Jesus enters the temple,

takes possession of it

and will live in the Eucharist until the end of time.

Once we have known our vocation,

we must follow it

and live it faithfully until we are called to heaven.

Reflection and Resolution

Prayer:

O God, you sent the Holy Spirit upon the apostles

as they were united in prayer with Mary,

the Mother of Jesus.

May the Queen of Apostles,

the same Mother of us all,

help us to serve your majesty faithfully,

and to spread the glory of Your Name

by word and example.

Through Christ our Lord.

Amen.

"Our Father..."

"Hail Mary..."

"Glory be..."

Queen of Apostles,

pray for us.

DAY SIX

"Standing near the cross of Jesus were his mother,

and his mother's sister,

Mary the wife of Clopas,

and Mary Magdalene" (Jn 19:25).

Let us look at Jesus,

He sacrificed himself on the cross.

Let us look at Mary,

she shared Christ's mission and passion with Him.

The essence of the redemption is on Calvary,

Jesus offers himself;

Mary offers herself and her Son,

whom she loves more than herself.

Jesus is the Redeemer;

Mary, the co-redemptrix.

Reflection and Resolution

Prayer:

O God, you sent the Holy Spirit upon the apostles

as they were united in prayer with Mary,

the Mother of Jesus.

May the Queen of Apostles,

the same Mother of us all,

help us to serve your majesty faithfully,

and to spread the glory of Your Name

by word and example.

Through Christ our Lord.

Amen.

"Our Father..."

"Hail Mary..."

"Glory be..."

Queen of Apostles,

pray for us.

DAY SEVEN

"When Jesus saw his mother and the disciple

whom he loved standing beside her,

he said to his mother,

'Woman, here is your son.'

Then He said to the disciple,

'Here is your mother'" (Jn 19:26-27).

When human perversity had reached its height

and had brought about the death of our Lord;

when the Shepherd was smitten

and the entire flock

of apostles and faithful were dispersed,

Jesus Christ offered hope,

salvation, his Mother:

"Here is your mother" (Jn 19:26).

Reflection and Resolution

Prayer:

O God, you sent the Holy Spirit upon the apostles

as they were united in prayer with Mary,

the Mother of Jesus.

May the Queen of Apostles,

the same Mother of us all,

help us to serve your majesty faithfully,

and to spread the glory of Your Name

by word and example.

Through Christ our Lord.

Amen.

"Our Father..."

"Hail Mary..."

"Glory be..."

Queen of Apostles,

pray for us.

DAY EIGHT

"All these were constantly devoting themselves to prayer,

together with certain women,

including Mary the mother of Jesus,

as well as his brothers" (Acts 1:14).

It is clear that we have to consider

and follow Mary as our model.

She is the most holy Virgin,

the co-redemptrix and the Queen of Apostles.

She offered Jesus on Calvary,

and together with the apostles

she prayed in the cenacle to obtain the Holy Spirit.

She took care of the Church,

newly born and already persecuted.

As Mother of the Church,

she became the outstanding member

of the Mystical Body of Christ.

Reflection and Resolution

Prayer:

O God, you sent the Holy Spirit upon the apostles

as they were united in prayer with Mary,

the Mother of Jesus.

May the Queen of Apostles,

the same Mother of us all,

help us to serve your majesty faithfully,

and to spread the glory of Your Name

by word and example.

Through Christ our Lord.

Amen.

"Our Father..."

"Hail Mary..."

"Glory be..."

Queen of Apostles,

pray for us.

DAY NINE

"Mary Immaculate,

the ever-virgin Mother of God,

having finished the course of her earthly life,

was assumed body and soul into heavenly glory" (Pius XII, November, 1950).

After the death of her Son, Jesus,

Mary took care of the apostles,

especially St. John, the youngest.

She accompanied them with her prayers,

good example and maternal comfort.

Thus, Jesus willed that Mary

be with them during their first years of evangelization,

as she had accompanied him.

After her earthly pilgrimage,

her mission fulfilled,

she was assumed into heaven.

Let us think about the last day of the world.

All the elect will gloriously enter heaven,

body and soul;

thus they will have an eternal reward.

Reflection and Resolution

Prayer:

O God, you sent the Holy Spirit upon the apostles

as they were united in prayer with Mary,

the Mother of Jesus.

May the Queen of Apostles,

the same Mother of us all,

help us to serve your majesty faithfully,

and to spread the glory of Your Name

by word and example.

Through Christ our Lord.

Amen.

"Our Father..."

"Hail Mary..."

"Glory be..."

Queen of Apostles,

pray for us.

NOVENA TO MARY, QUEEN OF ALL HEARTS

O Mary, Queen of All Hearts,

Advocate of the most hopeless cases;

Mother most pure, most compassionate;

Mother of Divine Love,

full of divine light,

we confide to your care the favors which we ask of you today.

Consider our misery, our tears,

our interior trials and sufferings!

We know that you can help us

through the merits of your Divine Son, Jesus.

We promise, if our prayers are heard,

to spread your glory,

by making you known under the title of

Mary, Queen of the Universe.

Grant, we beseech you,

hear our prayers,

for every day you give us so many proofs of your love

and your power of intercession to heal both body and soul.

We hope against all hope:

Ask Jesus to cure us, pardon us,

and grant us final perseverance.

O Mary, Queen of all Hearts, help us,

we have confidence in you. (3 times)

NOVENA TO OUR GUARDIAN ANGEL #1

Prayer

O most faithful companion,

appointed by God to be my guardian,

and who never leaves my side,

how shall I thank you for your faithfulness and love

and for the benefits which you have obtained for me!

You watch over me when I sleep;

you comfort me when I am sad;

you avert the dangers that threaten me

and warn me of those to come;

you withdraw me from sin

and inspire me to good;

you exhort me to penance when I fall

and reconcile me to God.

I beg you not to leave me.

Comfort me in adversity,

restrain me in prosperity,

defend me in danger,

and assist me in temptations,

lest at any time I fall beneath them.

Offer up in the sight of the Divine Majesty

my prayers and petitions,

and all my works of piety,

and help me to persevere in grace

until I come to everlasting life.

Amen.

NOVENA TO OUR GUARDIAN ANGEL #2

O holy angels, whom God,

by the effect of His goodness and His tender regard for my welfare,

has charged with the care of my conduct,

and who assists me in all my wants

and comforts me in all my afflictions,

who supports me when I am discouraged

and continually obtains for me new favors,

I return thee profound thanks,

and I earnestly beseech thee,

O most amiable protector,

to continue thy charitable care and defense of me

against the malignant attacks of all my enemies.

Keep me away from all occasions of sin.

Obtain for me the grace of listening attentively

to thy holy inspirations

and of faithfully putting them into practice.

In particular, I implore thee to obtain for me

the favor which I ask for by this novena.

[Here mention your need(s).]

Protect me in all the temptations and trials of this life,

but more especially at the hour of my death,

and do not leave me until thou hast conducted me

into the presence of my Creator

in the mansions of everlasting happiness.

Amen.

NOVENA TO OUR LADY OF PEACE

To Mary, Our Lady Of Sorrows

Most holy and afflicted Virgin, Queen of Martyrs,

you stood beneath the cross,

witnessing the agony of your dying Son.

Look with a mother's tenderness and pity on us,

as we kneel before you.

We venerate your sorrows,

and place our request with dutiful confidence

in the sanctuary of your wounded heart.

Present them, we beseech you,

on our behalf to Jesus Christ,

through the merits of His own most Sacred Passion and Death,

together with your sufferings at the foot of the cross.

Through the united efficacy of both,

obtain the granting of our petition.

To whom shall we have recourse in our wants and miseries

if not to you, Mother of Mercy?

You have drunk so deeply of the chalice of your Son,

you can with compassion receive our sorrows.

Holy Mary, your soul was pierced by a sword of sorrow

at the sight of the passion of your Divine Son.

Intercede for us and obtain from Jesus these petitions

if they be for His honor and glory

and for our good and the good of our nation.

That our nation's leaders remove those U.S. Marshals who guard abortion chambers and station them on airplanes to protect innocent travelers,

Our Lady of Sorrows, hear us.

That our president may call for a moratorium on abortion while the war against terrorism is waged,

Our Lady of Sorrows, hear us.

That all those injured in the terrorist attacks recover quickly,

Our Lady of Sorrows, hear us.

That the souls of the departed rest in the eternal peace of your Crucified Son, Jesus Christ,

Our Lady of Sorrows, hear us.

That the families of all those lost in the terrorist attack may know the comfort of Christ's constant love,

Our Lady of Sorrows, hear us.

That the parents, grandparents and health care professionals who kill the innocent by abortion may receive the strength to seek Christ's forgiveness,

Our Lady of Sorrows, hear us.

That the biologists, scientists, pharmaceutical company executives, medical school professors and others who are involved in the daily killing of the preborn may recognize the evil they perpetrate, and repent,

Our Lady of Sorrows, hears us.

That our soldiers, firefighters, policeman, and medical personnel will be protected by the grace of God,

Our Lady of Sorrows, hear us.

Amen.

NOVENA TO OUR LADY OF AMERICA

DAY ONE

Our Lady of America,

you asked that the United States of America

"be the country dedicated to my purity"

and that your children in America

"be the children of my Pure Heart."

Please intercede for us

that we may be granted this grace

and morally good leaders who will act

according to the revealed will of God

and the foundational principles

of the Declaration of Independence

and the Constitution of the United States of America.

DAY TWO

Our Lady of America, you said,

"I desire, through my children of America,

to further the cause of faith

and purity among peoples and nations.

Let them come to me with confidence and simplicity,

and I, their Mother,

will teach them to become pure like to my Heart

that their own hearts may be more pleasing to the Heart of my Son."

Please intercede for us

that we may be granted this grace

and morally good leaders who will act

according to the revealed will of God

and the foundational principles

of the Declaration of Independence

and the Constitution of the United States of America.

DAY THREE

Our Lady of America, you said,

"What I ask, have asked, and will continue to ask

is reformation of life.

There must be sanctification from within.

I will work my miracles of grace

only in those who ask for them

and empty their souls of the love and attachment to sin

and all that is displeasing to my Son."

Please intercede for us

that we may be granted this grace

and morally good leaders who will act

according to the revealed will of God

and the foundational principles

of the Declaration of Independence

and the Constitution of the United States of America.

DAY FOUR

Our Lady of America, you said,

"My dear children,

either you will do as I desire and reform your lives,

or God Himself will need to cleanse you

in the fires of untold punishment.

You must be prepared to receive His great gift of peace."

Please intercede for us

that we may be granted this grace

and morally good leaders who will act

according to the revealed will of God

and the foundational principles

of the Declaration of Independence

and the Constitution of the United States of America.

DAY FIVE

Our Lady of America, you said,

"It is the wish of my Son

that fathers and mothers strive to imitate me

and my chaste spouse in our holy life at Nazareth.

We practiced the simple virtues of family life,

Jesus our Son being the center of all our love and activity.

The Holy Trinity dwelt with us

in a manner far surpassing anything that can ever be imagined.

For ours was the earthly paradise

where once again God walked among men."...

"The Divine Trinity will dwell in your midst

only if you are faithful in practicing the virtues

of our life at Nazareth.

Then, you also, my children,

you also will become another paradise.

God will then walk among you and you will have peace."

Please intercede for us

that we may be granted this grace

and morally good leaders who will act

according to the revealed will of God

and the foundational principles

of the Declaration of Independence

and the Constitution of the United States of America.

DAY SIX

Our Lady of America,

you asked your beloved sons, the priests,

"to practice self-denial and penance in a special manner,

because it is you who must lead my children in the way of peace...

Thus, by sanctification from within you,

you will become a bright and burning light to the faithful,

who look to you for help and guidance."

Please intercede for us

that we may be granted this grace

and morally good leaders who will act

according to the revealed will of God

and the foundational principles

of the Declaration of Independence

and the Constitution of the United States of America.

DAY SEVEN

Our Lady of America,

you asked that the youth of our nation

be the leaders of a movement of renewal

on the face of the earth.

You asked that they be prepared by instilling into them,

not only the knowledge of the Divine Indwelling,

but a serious study of it,

living it in such a way that the Divine Presence becomes,

as it were an intimate and necessary part of their life and daily living.

From this will flow a great love,

a conflagration that will envelop the world

in the flames of Divine Charity."

Please intercede for us

that we may be granted this grace

and morally good leaders who will act

according to the revealed will of God

and the foundational principles

of the Declaration of Independence

and the Constitution of the United States of America.

DAY EIGHT

Our Lady of America,

you said that those who wear your medal

"with great faith and fervent devotion to you

will receive the grace of intense purity of heart

and the particular love of the Holy Virgin and her Divine Son."

You also said,

'Sinners will receive the grace of repentance

and the spiritual strength to live as true children of Mary.

As in life, so in death,

this blessed medal will be as a shield to protect them

against the evil spirits,

and St. Michael himself will be at their side

to allay their fears at the final hour."

Please intercede for us

that we may be granted this grace

and morally good leaders who will act

according to the revealed will of God

and the foundational principles

of the Declaration of Independence

and the Constitution of the United States of America.

DAY NINE

Our Lady of America,

you asked that a statue be made in your image and placed,

after being solemnly carried in procession,

in the Basilica of the National Shrine

of the Immaculate Conception in Washington, D.C.

You said that you wished to be honored there

in a special way as Our Lady of America,

the Immaculate Virgin.

You promised that the placement of your statue in the Shrine

would be a special safeguard for our country.

Please intercede for us

that we may be granted this grace

and morally good leaders who will act

according to the revealed will of God

and the foundational principles

of the Declaration of Independence

and the Constitution of the United States of America.

(The following prayer is said each day after the above prayer is completed.)

PRAYER OF SISTER MILDRED TO OUR LADY OF AMERICA

O Immaculate Mother, Queen of our Country,

open our hearts, our homes,

and our Land to the coming of Jesus, your Divine Son.

With Him, reign over us, O heavenly Lady,

so pure and so bright

with the radiance of God's light shining in and about you.

Be our Leader against the powers of evil

set upon wresting the world of souls,

redeemed at such a great cost

by the sufferings of your Son and of yourself,

in union with Him, from that same Savior,

Who loves us with infinite charity.

We gather about you, O chaste and holy Mother,

Virgin Immaculate, Patroness of our beloved Land,

determined to fight under your banner of holy purity

against the wickedness that would make all the world an abyss of evil,

without God and without your loving maternal care.

We consecrate our hearts, our homes,

our Land to your Most Pure Heart, O great Queen,

that the kingdom of your Son,

our Redeemer and our God,

may be firmly established in us.

We ask no special sign of you, sweet Mother,

for we believe in your great love for us,

and we place in you our entire confidence.

We promise to honor you by faith, love,

and the purity of our lives according to your desire.

Reign over us, then, O Virgin Immaculate,

with your Son Jesus Christ.

May His Divine Heart and your most chaste Heart

be ever enthroned and glorified among us.

Use us, your children of America,

as your instruments in bringing peace among men and nations.

Work your miracles of grace in us,

so that we may be a glory to the Blessed Trinity,

Who created, redeemed, and sanctifies us.

May your valiant Spouse, St. Joseph,

with the holy Angels and Saints,

assist you and us in "renewing the face of the earth."

Then when our work is over,

come, Holy Immaculate Mother,

and as our Victorious Queen,

lead us to the eternal kingdom,

where your Son reigns forever as King.

Amen.

Our Father...

Hail Mary... and

Glory Be...

By thy holy and Immaculate Conception, O Mary,

deliver us from evil!

NOVENA TO OUR LADY OF FATIMA

Recite this prayer for 9 days...

Most Holy Virgin,

who has deigned to come to Fatima

to reveal to the three little shepherds

the treasures of graces hidden in the recitation of the Rosary,

inspire our hearts with a sincere love of this devotion,

so that by meditating on the mysteries

of our redemption that are recalled in it,

we may gather the fruits

and obtain the conversion of sinners,

the conversion of Russia,

and this favor that I so earnestly seek....

(State your request here...)

which I ask of you in this novena,

for the greater glory of God,

for your own honor,

and for the good of all people.

Amen,

Recite the following prayers...

3 Our Father...

3 Hail Marys...

3 Glory Be...

OUR LADY OF GOOD REMEDY

(Feast on October 8 th.)

O Queen of Heaven and earth,

most Holy Virgin,

we venerate thee.

Thou art the beloved daughter

of the Most High God,

the chosen mother of the Incarnate Word,

the immaculate spouse of the Holy Spirit,

the sacred vessel of the Most Holy Trinity.

O Mother of the Divine Redeemer,

who under the title of

Our Lady of Good Remedy

comes to the aid of all

who call upon thee,

extend thy maternal protection to us.

We depend on thee,

dear Mother,

as helpless and needy children

depend on a tender and caring mother.

Pray the Hail Mary...

O Lady of Good Remedy,

source of unfailing help,

grant that we may draw

from thy treasury of graces

in our time of need.

Touch the hearts of sinners,

that they may seek

reconciliation and forgiveness.

Bring comfort to

the afflicted and the lonely;

help the poor and the hopeless;

aid the sick and the suffering.

May they be healed in body

and strengthened in spirit

to endure their sufferings

with patient resignation

and Christian fortitude.

Pray the Hail Mary...

Dear Lady of Good Remedy,

source of unfailing help,

thy compassionate heart knows a remedy

for every affliction and misery

we encounter in life.

Help me with thy prayers and intercession

to find a remedy for my problems and needs,

especially for...

(State your special intentions here.)

On my part,

O loving Mother,

I pledge myself to a more intensely Christian lifestyle,

to a more careful observance of the laws of God,

to be more conscientious

in fulfilling the obligations of my state in life,

and to strive to be a source of healing

in this broken world of ours.

Dear Lady of Good Remedy,

be ever present to me,

and through thy intercession,

may I enjoy health of body and peace of mind,

and grow stronger in the faith

and in the love of thy Son, Jesus.

Pray the Hail Mary...

V. Pray for us, O Holy Mother of Good Remedy,

R. That we may deepen our dedication to thy Son,

and make the world alive with His Spirit.

Manufactured by Amazon.ca
Acheson, AB

11279701R00177